BRIDGING THE TAX GAP

D1457952

Economic
Policy
Institute

About the Editor

Max Sawicky is institute economist at the Economic Policy Institute. He is a member of the National Executive Board of Americans for Democratic Action and the editorial board of Working USA. He also runs the Weblog MaxSpeak at www.maxspeak.org/mt.

About the Authors

Donald C. Alexander is a partner in the law firm of Akim, Gump, Strauss, Hauer, and Feld. He served from 1973 to 1977 as commissioner of the Internal Revenue Service, from 1984 to 1989 as director of the U.S. Chamber of Commerce, and from 1993 to 1996 as a commissioner of the Martin Luther King Jr. Federal Holiday Commission.

Reuven S. Avi-Yonah is the Irwin I. Cohn Professor of Law and director of the International Tax LLM program at the University of Michigan. He is a graduate of the Hebrew University (B.A. 1983, summa cum laude), Harvard University (Ph.D. in history, 1986), and Harvard Law School (J.D. 1989, magna cum laude). He is married with two children and lives in Ann Arbor, Michigan.

Sheldon S. Cohen was a partner in the law firm of Morgan, Lewis & Bockius. He served as chief counsel of the Internal Revenue Service in 1964, and as commissioner of the Internal Revenue Service from 1965 to 1969.

Joseph H. Guttentag was deputy assistant secretary for international tax affairs in the Clinton Treasury. Previously, he was a senior tax partner in the law firm of Arnold & Porter in Washington, D.C. and Tokyo. He served as chairman of the Fiscal Committee of the Organization for Economic Cooperation and Development in Paris and as chair of the international tax groups of the U.S. Chamber of Commerce, the American Chamber of Commerce in Japan, and the American Bar Association.

Wojciech Kopczuk is associate professor of economics at Columbia University and faculty research fellow at the National Bureau of Economic Research. He obtained his Ph.D from the University of Michigan in 2001 and has published articles in leading academic journals on topics such as estate taxation, wealth inequality, tax avoidance, and the cost of income taxation.

Robert S. McIntyre is director of Citizens for Tax Justice. For the past three decades, he has helped lead the fight for fair and adequate taxes at the federal, state, and local levels.

BRIDGING THE TAX GAP

Addressing the Crisis in Federal Tax Administration

Max B. Sawicky, editor

Economic
Policy
Institute

For Allegra, who will conquer algebra!

The views expressed by individual authors in this volume are not necessarily those of the Economic Policy Institute.

Table of contents

Acknowledgments

This book is the culmination of a project that benefited from the advice of leading scholars and practitioners in the field of tax administration. We would like to thank Henry J. Aaron, Donald C. Alexander, Reuven S. Avi-Yonah, Leonard E. Burman, Sheldon S. Cohen, Joseph Guttentag, Wojciech Kopczuk, Robert Kuttner, Robert S. McIntyre, Ronald A. Pearlman, Charles O. Rossotti, and Eric Toder for their assistance. They are of course not responsible for the views expressed here.

We would also like to commend Rebecca Ray and Ellen Levy of the Economic Policy Institute for valuable assistance in preparing the interview transcripts.

We are grateful to the Popplestone Foundation for its generous support of this project.

Other recent books from the Economic Policy Institute

The State of Working America 2004/2005
Lawrence Mishel, Jared Bernstein, & Sylivia Allegretto

Rethinging Growth Strategies: How State and Local Taxes and Services Affect Economic Development
Robert G. Lynch

Retirement Income: The Crucial Role of Social Security
Christian Weller and Edward N. Wolff

Also by Max B. Sawicky

The End of Welfare? Consequences of Federal Devolution for the Nation
Max B. Sawicky, editor

Risky Business: Private Management of Public Schools
Craig E. Richards, Rima Shore, & Max B. Sawicky

Executive Summary

The ability to finance public services at a low financial cost with minimal social dislocation is a precious national asset. The United States is blessed by a tax system with these attributes—the vast bulk of taxes owed are paid voluntarily and on time. In a $13 trillion economy, our federal government taxing authority costs about $10 billion—less than one dollar out of a thousand—to run. A nation squanders such an asset at its peril, but that is what is happening now.

Compliance with the federal tax system is eroding. The Internal Revenue Service estimates that as much as $350 billion in taxes are not paid voluntarily and timely. On a bare-bones enforcement budget, about $50 billion is eventually recovered. The remaining gap means that tax rates must be higher than necessary to collect the revenue that comes in, and moreover, that such rates penalize the honest taxpayer for the sake of the evader. The absence of a tax cop on the beat demoralizes those who pay their correct amount and encourages evasion, further adding to the enforcement burden and the revenue loss.

Current federal deficit levels are widely recognized to be unsustainable in the long run. The Bush Administration has proposed and ratified spending increases as rapid as any presidential administration in history, and it has added to future spending with a new, unfunded prescription drug benefit under Medicare. In about a dozen years, the Social Security program will begin to require cash transfers from general revenue. Tax cuts of the past four years have made an untenable situation worse, rather than better. Under all plausible circumstances, tax increases will force their way back onto the policy agenda. One important leavening factor will be the willingness of policy makers to improve enforcement of taxes already owed, not just the legislation of literal tax increases.

This book provides a survey of the compliance problem in language the non-expert can understand. We also discuss a broad gamut of remedies. Contributors to this volume include eminent practitioners in the field of tax enforcement, as well as scholars in tax policy.

The opening chapter by Max B. Sawicky provides a comprehensive overview of the topic. It begins by summarizing research on the extent of non-compliance, and on the magnitudes of potential pay-offs from more vigorous enforcement measures. It includes a critique of policies that have debilitated the Internal Revenue Service, which include excessive constraints on IRS personnel, inadequate funding, increasing complexity in the tax code, misplaced focus on low-income taxpayers, and unsuccessful technology modernization. It also surveys possible remedies.

The second and third chapters feature interviews with former commissioners of the Internal Revenue Service.

Sheldon Cohen worked for the IRS in the 1950s and served as commissioner under President Lyndon Johnson. Cohen describes the process of building the modern IRS and the problems in running it.

Donald Alexander served as commissioner under President Richard Nixon in the 1970s. He discusses the shortcomings of potential tax reforms from the standpoint of tax administration. He also provides a window into the political pressures facing the IRS.

Robert McIntyre describes the burgeoning business in illicit tax shelters. Limited IRS resources place the government at an increasing disadvantage in dealing with wealthy taxpayers who can afford to buy expert tax planning that amounts to custom-made tax-cut schemes tailored to the individual. These schemes typically dance back and forth across the boundary of the law, but the issues raised are sufficiently complex as to permit guilty parties to win compromises from the government, rather than pay their rightful share of tax.

Joseph Guttentag and Reuven Avi-Yonah lay out the increasing difficulties of levying the income tax in a globalizing world economy. They reveal some of the mechanisms of high-level tax evasion and propose remedies to recover the huge sums lost to off-shore financial shenanigans.

Finally, Professor Wojciech Kopczuk argues that tax simplification could ease the enforcement problem and, to some extent, preclude the need for heightened enforcement measures. He reviews research on the determinants of tax compliance behavior, and he evaluates alternative strategies to improve compliance from the standpoint of equity and economic efficiency.

The aim of this volume is to alert policy makers to the growing problem of tax compliance, and to feasible solutions. The costs of inaction are great, but so too are the potential rewards of reform. Alternatives to closing the budget deficit are usually unpleasant. When the day comes that the Congress decides to face up to its fiscal responsibilities, it will find that increasing the rate at which taxes are paid voluntarily and on time is one of the best deals we can get in economic policy.

CHAPTER 1

Do-it-yourself tax cuts: The crisis in U.S. tax enforcement

by Max B. Sawicky

According to the latest estimates, as much as $353 billion in taxes—
16% of the total owed—went unpaid in 2001. If we ranked states in
order of aggregate individual income tax liability, this "tax gap" would
far exceed total federal taxes paid by the residents of any single U.S.
state or even the total taxes paid by all 29 states with the lowest total
tax liability combined.

More importantly, recovery of unpaid taxes could significantly reduce projected federal budget deficits over the next 10 years. Burgeoning budget problems (Sawicky 2005; Price and Sawicky 2004) and the
associated difficulties of enacting tax increases make closing the tax
gap a salient political issue and an important policy priority. Indeed,
one reason to resist tax increases is the knowledge that many tax
payers are escaping their own tax obligations.

This chapter provides an overview of what former commissioner of
the Internal Revenue Service (IRS) Charles O. Rossotti called "the crisis in tax administration" (Rossotti 2002; quoted in Aaron and Slemrod
2004), and it discusses some remedies to address this problem.[1]

The tax gap

For fiscal year 2005, over $2 trillion in federal taxes will be col-
lected. The budget of the Internal Revenue Service is about $10
billion. To a great extent, U.S. tax collections benefit from widespread, voluntary compliance with the tax code. The extent of this
compliance lifts an enormous burden from government.

Of course, to some extent the voluntarism is not an act of civic-mindedness, but instead inspired by a desire to avert the threat of IRS enforcement measures. In this sense, the slim $10 billion spent by the IRS has some ripple effect on taxpayers who never directly run afoul of tax collecting authorities. The estimated effect amounts to $12 of regular tax payments for every dollar collected through an audit.

Even so, estimates of taxes owed but not paid are significant. As noted above, unpaid taxes in 2001 range between an estimated $312 billion and $353 billion, as opposed to $1,767 billion paid "voluntarily and timely." (All estimates are in dollars and do not necessarily reflect proportions of taxpayer types.) Payments made late and because of enforcement measures closed the gap by $55 billion, for a net of $257 to $298 billion in missing money. These numbers do not include illegal activities in the underground economy, but they do reflect taxes due on otherwise legal economic transactions, such as "working off the books."

Until recently, a leading concern in tax enforcement has been the quality of data available to the authorities. Information on the sources of non-compliance enables the IRS to target potential evasion and better allocate its extremely limited resources.

For nearly two decades, the IRS has been limited to data on taxpayers collected for tax years 1979, 1982, 1985, and 1988. This resulted from auditing a representative sample of taxpayers, in addition to other audits and research. In general the operating assumption has been that the pattern of non-compliance is unchanging since 1988, an assumption virtually certain to be wrong, but nevertheless the best benchmark possible in the absence of more current data.

At the time of this writing, new information about compliance is just becoming available to the IRS in the form of the IRS National Research Project (NRP). The range of the tax gap reported above is a preliminary NRP finding. The latest findings are in the same ballpark as those based on 16-year-old information, but there is a disturbing increase in the noncompliance rate for 2001—the tax gap divided by total estimated taxes owed. The rate rises from 14.9% (based on 1988 data) to as much as 16.6% (based on the most recent data), roughly an 11% increase. Among individual taxpayers alone (as opposed to corporations or businesses paying payroll tax), the upper bound of possible growth in noncompliance in the latest data is 25%.

The NRP's focus is on measuring underreporting in the individual income tax. Research on corporations, partnerships, and other types of taxpayers will come later, notwithstanding the high rates of non-compliance that can be found among these groups.

Components of the tax gap

Most of the tax gap—$250 billion to $292 billion—is founded on the underreporting of net income (i.e., reporting too little income and/or too many deductions). A smaller portion of this tax gap is due to non-filing ($30 billion) and underpayment ($32 billion). Nearly all of the estimated non-filing and underpayment pertains to the individual income tax.

In the underreporting category, the taxes most often underreported are: individual income (between $150 billion and $187 billion), corporate income ($30 billion), payroll ($66 billion to $71 billion), and estate and excise ($4 billion).

Within the income tax category, about half of the gap is due to underreporting of business net income. Lesser shares are due to underreporting of non-business income, and less still to incorrect reporting of deductions, exemptions, adjustments, and credits ($25 billion). In the payroll tax category, the bulk of non-compliance is attributed to the self-employed ($51 billion to $56 billion).

Confidence in these estimates varies, given the spotty character of available data and the idiosyncratic difficulties in analyzing assorted components of the gap. Estimates of the largest pieces— underreporting of business income, corporate income, and self-employment income—used to be considered the less-reliable estimates; presumably with the new NRP data, confidence has improved.

Considered in terms of the percentage of dollars lost by tax category, the three leading categories are self-employment tax (nearly 60%), corporate income tax (over 40%), and the estate tax (over 20%).

Another breakdown is by "visibility" categories within the individual income tax. The vast bulk of underreporting is attributed to nonfarm proprietors, rents and royalties, farm income, and informal suppliers ("proprietors who operate in an informal business style," which includes street merchants and the like), among other areas. These types of taxpayers are required to conduct "little or no information reporting" of their financial affairs (Plumley 2004).

One way to consider the extent of unreported income is to compare data from the Internal Revenue Service with other sources. The Bureau of Economic Analysis of the U.S. Department of Commerce prepares data on the national economy in the National Income and Product Accounts (NIPA). This includes estimates of the "AGI Gap," which is the difference between adjusted gross income measures implied by returns filed with the IRS and the income level data gathered by other sources. **Figure A** shows the extent of discrepancies by type of taxable income. The total for 2002 exceeded $900 billion.

Leading enforcement problems

A basic distinction in tax enforcement is that between *evasion* and *avoidance.* Evasion pertains to illegal under- or non-payment of taxes. Avoidance refers to legal rearrangement of one's financial affairs to reduce or eliminate tax liability. In the many areas where the law is vague, owing to the complexity of the issue, the line between evasion and avoidance can be difficult to trace. The general intent of the law is to deny tax benefits to transactions or arrangements motivated solely by tax considerations, but spelling out that aim in practice is daunting. This overview is mostly concerned with evasion.

Tip of the iceberg: the Earned Income Tax Credit

One of the most talked-about lapses in tax compliance is unjustified claims for the Earned Income Tax Credit (EITC) (Sawicky 2002). The EITC is a refundable tax credit available to workers with low incomes. A narrow concern with the EITC could not possibly be justified by worries over insufficient total revenue collections. In the context of the program itself, EITC over-claims of approximately $9 billion are significant, yet they are but one minor share of the overall tax gap. Much taxpayer confusion afflicts all of the tax benefits for children, such as the dependent exemption, because the eligibility rules are so complex. Returns from improved tax enforcement surely can be found in many other places as well.

FIGURE A   The "AGI Gap," 2002

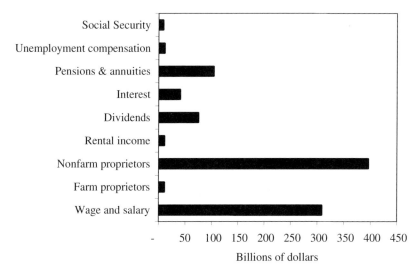

Source: *Survey of Current Business.*

Non-compliance under the EITC does not necessarily signify dishonesty. The data do not reveal who is consciously cheating and who is not. They do show, however, that the complexity of the EITC often provokes claims for too little a credit, as well as for too much (Wasow 2002). In fact, a recent study found that about four in every 10 low-income taxpayers had never heard of the EITC (Maag 2005). For such taxpayers employing professional preparers, their lack of knowledge did not prevent them from applying for the benefit, but given such a common lack of knowledge, it should not be surprising that some persons file incorrect claims for the credit.

The IRS is instituting elaborate, extraordinary enforcement measures directed at EITC compliance, raising questions about fairness in the targeting of enforcement efforts. In 2003, the IRS requested a 69% increase in funds for EITC enforcement but only a 3% increase for enforcement in all other areas (Burman 2003).

Tax shelters

In contrast to low-income persons filing over-claims for the EITC, the typical abusers of corporate tax shelters are likely to understand their tax obligations very well. Estimates of losses from underreporting by corporations are $30 billion for 2001, of which tax shelters accounted for between $10 billion and $15 billion annually (Stratton 2005).

What is a tax shelter? In the current income tax system, tax rates can vary according to the type of income, the type of asset generating the income, the form of legal organization of the business firm, the manner in which business investment is financed, and a host of other factors. For individuals and business firms with complex financial affairs, there is usually flexibility in how to organize or account for these activities. A basic means of tax minimization is to receive income under circumstances in which tax rates are low, or absent, and to structure deductions where tax rates (hence the values of the deductions) are high.

In some circumstances "tax planning" of this type is permitted by law, while in others it stretches what the law allows, and in others still it can be in blatant violation of the rules.

Litigation is a key IRS tool in combating abuse, but since it is expensive, resolution of non-compliance allegations is often based on compromise rather than strict judgment of guilt or innocence.

Increasing workloads, decreasing staff, the statute of limitations, and the "hazards" (uncertainties and costs) of litigation put pressure on the IRS to settle out of court. Taxpayers are likely to anticipate higher net benefits from tax litigation than the IRS, putting downward pressure on the amount of any out-of-court settlements (Plumley 2004).

The government cannot afford to investigate and pursue every case to a judicial conclusion. In effect, there is an incentive for well-heeled corporations and individuals to make aggressive claims in their returns, banking on the IRS seeking other enforcement targets, or on using their legal resources to win major concessions from the under-staffed, underfunded authorities.

A current case illustrates another dilemma in shelter prosecution. Leaders of the KPMG accounting firm's tax practice have been indicted for shelter abuse, and the company itself was penalized. At the same time, harsher prosecution and penalties would have been possible, but the federal government was reluctant to begin a process that could have destroyed the firm. Evidently, in the wake of the demise of the Enron-implicated Arthur Anderson organization, a large firm with many employees may enjoy the protection of a "too big to fail" presumption.

International transactions

Transactions involving foreign countries magnify two dimensions of the tax enforcement burden. One is the added complexity of tax law applying to multinational corporations and cross-border transactions. Complexity and ambiguity in tax law facilitate tax shelter abuse.

A second is the added information burden on authorities, since the foreign side of transactions is more difficult for the IRS to monitor and investigate. Much tax collection from business firms relies on accurate and honest self-reporting of income and expenses. Tax havens with bank secrecy laws, whose financial institutions are patronized by U.S. taxpayers, raise obstacles to tax enforcement. In fact, compared to some Western European countries, the United States itself is something of a tax haven (Sullivan 2004).

Vito Tanzi, a tax expert and former official of the International Monetary Fund, has estimated that $7 trillion in assets generate income not reported to any nation's tax authorities. In 2001, Manhattan District Attorney Robert M. Morgenthau testified before the U.S. Senate that, among off-shore tax havens, Grand Cayman alone has $800 billion in U.S. dollar deposits, and that amount was increasing by $120 billion annually.

The real story on offshore wealth that has been spirited out to tax havens is the lack of solid information on the amount, the source, the ownership, and the legality of the activities that generated said wealth. The national security dimension of this problem in the wake of the terrorist attacks in 2001 has become obvious.

Former IRS Commissioner Charles O. Rossotti testified that the extent of lost revenue could be as much as $40 billion. IRS consultant Jack Blum suggested a higher lost revenue of $70 billion in 2002 alone (Sullivan 2004).

There is no shortage of business enterprises—including respectable ones with famous names—providing "wealth management services" to the rich, services that entail avoiding "unnecessary taxes." As for other enforcement matters, the amount of foregone revenue is only half of the concern. The integrity and fairness of the tax system affects the strength of voluntary compliance, without which the finances of the U.S. government would come crashing down.

Trusts, partnerships, and S-corporations

Trusts, partnerships, and S-corporations, also known as "pass-through entities," are organizations that stand between an individual or individuals and the income and losses being generated by a business firm or investment portfolio. They serve various legitimate purposes, but they are also used by some taxpayers to hide income or generate artificial losses to offset taxable income. These pass-through entities may serve no business purpose at all, other than to evade or legally reduce taxes.

"Small" businesses and the self-employed

The small business and the self-employed tax grouping is highly diverse, though its members are dealt with under a single branch of the IRS. It encompasses a wide range of incomes and stations, from street peddlers to corporate law practices. Partnerships and S-corporations might have relatively few employees, but 60% of income to such entities is received by taxpayers with $500,000 or more annual income (Slemrod 2004). By contrast, the incomes of sole proprietors resemble more the population at large. As noted above, the non-compliance rate for this group is extremely high—approaching 50%.

The tax enforcement problem is particularly acute for assorted subgroups in this category, although in different ways. At the low-income end, there are taxpayers who are not compelled to maintain detailed records of their business transactions, as well as those who are able to do business in cash. For many—especially in the case of farm income—"sole proprietor" incomes are negative and offset other taxable income. (Many such cases are part-time farmers.)

At the high end, in the case of partnerships and S-corporations, there are taxpayers with the resources to structure their activities in complex ways that walk the line between legal avoidance and illegal evasion.

In both cases, to an important extent paying taxes is done on the honor system, albeit under the shadow of possible IRS intervention.

The economies of enforcement are less favorable in this context as well. A given case may involve a minimal amount of recoverable taxes, relative to the costs of auditing and prosecuting tax evasion. Conversely, a given target of investigation may mobilize formidable legal resources in its defense.

Enforcement and the IRS

Expanded measures for enforcement of the tax code would be expected to pay for themselves in improved collections. Estimates of the extent of the payoff vary, depending on how enforcement is intensified. IRS Commissioner Mark Everson believes the benefit/cost ratio is more than four-to-one (Kenney 2005a), which means a dollar more for enforcement brings at least $4 back to the Treasury and a net $3 reduction in the budget deficit (or increase in the budget surplus). We noted at the outset of this chapter that the $10 billion IRS budget (which also goes to functions other than enforcement, such as taxpayer assistance, and processing over 130 million individual income tax returns) accounted for $56 billion in additional collections in 2001.

Of the taxes that remain unpaid, some underpayments are actually already known to the IRS, but the resources to recover this debt simply are not currently available. Former Deputy Assistant Secretary for Tax Policy Leonard Burman, citing former IRS Commissioner Charles Rossotti, estimated the known arrears to be $30 billion. In his view, this could have been recovered with an additional $2.2 billion in resources for enforcement.

Resources

There is little dispute that the workload of the IRS has been increasing more rapidly than its organizational capacity. The number of tax returns has increased steadily, partially due to a growing population and economy. There is also evidence, however, that returns have increased faster than population growth, in the form of more returns for un-married persons and for children. Another dimension adding to the increased IRS workload involves high-income persons and the growth of pass-through entities (as noted above). Still another factor straining IRS capacity is the multiplication of highly complex and specialized financial instruments. The estimated overall increase in workload between 1992 and 2002 is 16%.

The complexity of the tax code has increased by recent legislation. One example was the tax treatment of capital gains in 1997 legislation. A second example is the growth of benefits for education. A third is the increasing variety of tax-advantaged accounts for retirement. On the corporate income tax side, there are new provisions passed in 2004 aimed at promoting exports without violating World Trade Organization rules on discriminatory subsidies to industry.

The burden of increased enforcement tasks was further magnified by the diversion of IRS personnel away from enforcement and into other tasks. These included assisting taxpayers in return preparation; administering the expansions of refundable credits available under the individual income tax in 1993, 1997, and 2003; and regulating "527" political committees.

At the same time, IRS resources to finance personnel have *decreased* since 1992. The estimated reduction of "full-time equivalent" staff from 1992 to 2001 is 20,000 positions. Rossotti (2004) sums up as follows: "If the IRS staff grew by 2% per year through 2010, [then] the total staff would still be smaller than it was 20 years earlier (1990), while the economy is projected to be 86% larger and the tax system far more complex."

The IRS Oversight Board called for a 13% increase in the IRS budget for fiscal year 2006, 9% more than the Bush Administration budget proposal (Kenney 2005b).

Governance

In September 1997 and April 1998, the Senate Finance Committee under the chairmanship of William Roth (Rep.-Del.) held hearings on the practices of the Internal Revenue Service. Witnesses painted a black picture of an agency run amuck, trampling on the rights of honest taxpayers. The hearings provided a political launching pad for the Internal Revenue Service Restructuring and Reform Act, which among other provisions inaugurated a "Taxpayers Bill of Rights."

Subsequent investigation by the General Accounting Office—known now as the Government Accountability Office—resulted in a report not released to the public. This and other independent investigations found that testimony offered by witnesses at the hearings could not be substantiated (Donmoyer 2000).

In any case, the 1998 act tilted the playing field in tax disputes in favor of taxpayers suspected of non-compliance. The law also specifies misconduct that is grounds for IRS employee dismissal, known among IRS personnel as "the 10 deadly sins." The law further established a Treasury Inspector General for Tax Administration (TIGTA) with a mandate to investigate abuses by IRS staff. Oversight of the IRS by TIGTA, the Government Accountability Office, the Office of Management and Budget, and six Congressional committees consumes IRS resources (Rossotti 2004).

The question is the extent to which these new rules and administrative institutions block inappropriate practices by the IRS, as opposed to discouraging vigorous enforcement of the law in the legitimate pursuit of tax evasion.

An evaluation of the so-called "Taxpayer Bill of Rights" is beyond the scope of this analysis. What is clear is that the implied enforcement burden on the government has become heavier as a result.

Outsourcing

In contrast to the trend of regulating IRS personnel is the new initiative to contract out for collection of delinquent taxes. Legislation was passed in 2004 permitting the IRS to use private sector debt-collection agencies, which would be paid commissions of 25% of the amount of dollars recovered (Kenney 2005c). Concerns about possible abuse by IRS agents would presumably apply at least to the same extent to the private sector for-profit firms that are paid on the basis of how much money they retrieved. This experiment in tax collection has yet to be implemented.

Remedies

Document matching

The IRS is able to independently crosscheck taxpayer reporting of certain types of income—wage and salary, interest, dividends—under its "Information Returns Program" (IRP), which requires employers and financial institutions to report this information directly to the IRS. The use of computers is an obvious boon to this "document matching" function. If regulations for more comprehensive reporting of tax information by third parties can be established, such crosschecking could be even more valuable in collecting taxes.

Expanded document matching might also apply to deductions, as it does to some extent already. For instance, mortgage interest and state and local income and property tax liabilities are reported to the IRS by mortgagors and state governments, respectively. In the United Kingdom, non-profit institutions report charitable donations made in cash, facilitating their "return-free" system.

Another egregious gap in reporting pertains to capital gains. If brokers and mutual funds were required to report transactions to the tax authorities, taxpayers would probably not overstate their costs of assets purchased, known as "basis," with the current degree of impunity (Dodge and Soled 2005).

Complete coverage of such information may not be necessary for effective enforcement. Plumley (1996) suggests that because taxpayers cannot be certain whether their information is collected by the IRS from third parties, the risk-averse among them will act as if it has been collected and their compliance with tax obligations will be enhanced. Conversely, insofar as coverage approaches 100%, taxpayers will act under the certainty that the IRS computers will catch any discrepancies between information reported by them and by third parties.

The cost of crosschecking tax information is nearly negligible—about three cents—and the estimated payoff averages $21.00 (resulting in a revenue/cost ratio of 668-to-1).

Tax delinquency investigations (TDI)

When the IRS fails to receive a return from someone it has reason to believe is required to file, it sends a notice by mail. The reason could be that the taxpayer filed the previous year, or that a document match suggests a return ought to be filed. If there is no response to repeated TDI notices, further investigation can be triggered.

The benefit-to-cost ratio estimated for this device is very high (3,766-to-1). A TDI notice costs 31 cents, and the average return per dollar spent on notices is over $12,000.

Audits: enforcement and deterrent

There are audits, and then there are audits. The traditional process of a taxpayer reporting to an IRS field office, to subject himself and his personal or business records to detailed examination, is only one device. A second is known as the "correspondence audit," which entails a letter from the IRS to the taxpayer narrowly focused on specific questions about the person's tax return.

The "audit start rate" in 1991 was estimated at 0.65%. Raising it one percentage point to 1.65% would yield estimated annual net revenue of $56 billion. The average cost of an audit was $1,300. Its average yield was $71,000. As noted previously, by far the greater part of this is the indirect impact on taxpayer behavior on the part of those who are never themselves audited.

Over time, the audit rate has fallen significantly. In 1978 the overall rate for individuals was 2.15%; by 2001 it was 0.58%. From 1995 to 2001, the rate for business income fell from 4.0% to 2.0%. From 1993 to 2001, for corporations the rate fell from 3.0% to below 1.0%.

Since 1996, audits first took a deep dive, but then recovered to some extent. Individual audits fell from nearly two million in 1996 to about 600,000 by 2000, before climbing back to one million audits by 2004. High-income audits fell from 210,000 in 1996 to 92,000 in 2001, and then more than doubled to 195,000 by 2004. Criminal prosecutions have followed a similar pattern. By 1996 standards, the number of audits is still low, especially in light of growth in the scope of the task.

As a result of an increase in computer-generated correspondence audits (that is, instead of face-to-face audits), the increase in the overall audit rate for individual returned to 0.65% in 2003, up 14% from 2002 (TRAC 2005, cited in Kenney 2005b). Correspondence audits entail a notice sent to the taxpayer suggesting an error in the return and an invitation to rectify it without further penalty. The relevant question is the relative cost-effectiveness of alternative audit procedures, as well as other remedies.

Criminal prosecution

The most costly means of enforcement per case is actual prosecution of tax evaders. Prosecution yields net revenue gains, in terms of more honest reporting of tax information. Here again, the ripple effect is salient in two respects. Well-publicized indictments magnify the threat to others, and they may also raise confidence and voluntary compliance in general by assuring the public that the law is being applied vigorously to high-income persons.

In 1991, the average cost of a criminal conviction for tax evasion was $103,000, and the average returns in revenue were $1.7 million per conviction.

Property seizures, a prominent feature of IRS horror stories, are actually quite rare. The Treasury Inspector General for Tax Administration—charged with oversight of the IRS—reported that from May to September in 1999, there were 35 seizures in the United States, and all were conducted properly. The IRS was processing about 80 million returns annually in that period (Williams 2000).

Tax experts favoring stronger enforcement differ on the adequacy of the law in respect of abusive tax shelters. On one side is the view that legislation that clarifies what constitutes abuse would aid enforcement. Clarification in this context means specific definitions of where legitimate business purpose ends and tax-avoidance behavior begins. On the other hand, some feel that the lack of specificity in the law affords the authorities some flexibility in discouraging abuse. From this point of view, ingenious, highly-compensated attorneys, accountants, and economists can devise ways to circumvent any new law. More explicit language in law could give rise to the argument that anything not stipulated as out of bounds is automatically permissible.

There is no disagreement that more resources for investigation and prosecution, whatever the state of the law, would advance enforcement goals.

Tax preparation assistance

Filing an income tax return remains a complex task for many taxpayers. Computer software and tax preparation services make the job easier, but the IRS could expand its own assistance in this vein.

There already exists an industry of private-sector tax preparation services. Evidence of abuse by some of these service providers has led to suggestions of a need for regulation and perhaps licensing. Barbers and hair stylists often must be certified by boards, but there is no counterpart for tax preparers. Preparers serve both the "high-end" and the low, as far as taxpayer incomes are concerned. The IRS is concerned about high-end providers secretly marketing abusive tax shelter schemes, as well as about those serving low-income clients encouraging over-claims for the EITC.

There presently exists a network of non-profit tax assistance centers for low-income persons, largely staffed by volunteers. Expanding this network would have two, offsetting impacts on revenue. By increasing awareness of refundable credits available to low-income taxpayers, these centers would increase IRS cash refunds. At the same time, however, providing more accurate assistance in tax preparation could reduce over-claims for the EITC and other tax-based benefits for families with children. Over-claims are thought to account for roughly a third of the cost of the EITC, so it seems plausible that expansion of tax assistance to low-income persons would save more money than it would cost.

IRS assistance currently consists of answering questions by phone and providing direct assistance in preparation. An average cost of such activities per return was $14 in 1991, and the estimated revenue gain was $5,440.

The shift of IRS resources from enforcement to taxpayer assistance has inspired some criticism, since both activities arguably deserve to be expanded. Defenders of the shift may identify with the assertion of Rossotti: "I have never understood why anyone would think it is good business to fail to answer a phone call from someone who owed you money" (Rossotti 2004).

Withholding of tax at source

Employers are required to withhold individual income tax payments from their employees' wages and salaries. Discrepancies between total taxes paid and owed are settled when the worker files a return. There is no reason why such a practice could not be applied to interest and dividend income. Financial institutions could be required to withhold estimated tax.

For certain forms of consumption taxation, the taxpayer needs to calculate net saving for the tax year. Net saving is the difference between purchases (saving) and sales (dissaving) of financial assets. Given the multiplicity of assets and accounts held by some individuals, Aaron and Galper (1984) suggested the establishment of central asset management accounts. If all financial transactions are routed through a single account, the taxpayer is relieved of the need to calculate net saving, and the IRS has an independent source to verify capital income reported by the taxpayer. It might be possible to establish such accounts under the current tax system, to ease the compliance burden on the taxpayer and the enforcement burden on the government. Such accounts would also facilitate tax withholding.

International cooperation

Intergovernmental cooperation is required to enforce tax evasion that exploits cross-border transactions and nations functioning as tax havens. Such cooperation, at a minimum, entails the sharing of information among tax authorities in order to trace unreported income and verify information reported by taxpayers.

Law enforcement cooperation is also necessary. One egregious example is the case of some wealthy persons who sought to emigrate from the United States and establish citizenship elsewhere for the purpose of protecting from taxation their capital gains income accrued in the United States.

More ambitious would be efforts to harmonize tax systems among nations. Uniform definitions of net income would facilitate integration of tax enforcement efforts. If such coordination could be accomplished, greater uniformity of tax rates would discourage tax competition among nations and avoid the waste of economic resources caused by relocation of economic and financial activities according to tax considerations rather than business purposes.

The Organization for Economic Cooperation and Development (OECD) has taken up the problems of cross-border tax enforcement. Collaboration with the United States during the Clinton Administration was curbed in 2001 shortly after the election of George Bush. A conservative business coalition campaigned against the OECD's initiative under the banner of tax competition. The accusation was that cooperation in tax enforcement was aimed at penalizing low-tax nations who refused to raise their tax rates to those in Western Europe, with U.S. Rep. Nathan Deal (Rep.-Ga.) describing the arrangement as "fiscal European imperialism" (*Tax Notes* 2001).

In fact, the possibility of tax harmonization among the highly diverse tax systems of the OECD nations is close to nil. The most important priority for the OECD was information-sharing that would combat tax evasion. Criticism in this dimension rested on the debatable grounds of taxpayer privacy. The Bush Administration affirmed its opposition to tax evasion, but it also criticized the OECD posture as overly aggressive. Currently, the financial privacy laws of the United States, Switzerland, Luxembourg, Belgium, and Austria present obstacles to information sharing (Scott 2004). The terrorist attacks of September 11, 2001 led to only limited improvements (Sullivan 2004).

Tax simplification

Complex tax law is required at some level because the financial affairs of wealthy individuals and business firms can be complicated. At the same time, there are approaches to tax simplification that could reduce the compliance costs for taxpayers and ease the enforcement burden on the government.

For millions of taxpayers with modest or low incomes, taxes could be simplified to the point where filing a return became unnecessary. All tax liabilities could be met through an exact withholding system (Gale 2001).

Within the framework of the individual income tax, sets of provisions with similar purposes might be consolidated. One example is tax benefits for families with children (Cherry and Sawicky 2000). Another is the multiple opportunities for retirement savings accounts (Steuerle 1998). In a similar vein, the disparate treatment of different types of income—capital gains, dividends, and so-called "ordinary income" (i.e., wages and salaries and interest income)—could be eliminated in favor of all income being subject to the same set of tax rates. Multiple tax rates have little bearing on the complexity of a tax system; it is the definition of taxable income that creates the greatest compliance burden.

An especially burdensome facet of individual and corporate income taxes, as far as compliance is concerned, is the Alternative Minimum Tax (AMT). Given the expected growth in AMT coverage, the inescapable need for some kind of adjustment also will present an opportunity for reform. One obvious measure would be to replace the AMT with some kind of tighter cap on deductions.

More controversial are suggestions to transition from the current system, which has elements of both income and consumption taxation, to a full-blooded consumption tax. The chief argument here from the standpoint of simplification is that consumption is inherently simpler to measure than income. A shift towards consumption taxation could dramatically simplify rules pertaining to capital gains and depreciation. On the other hand, the transition between systems would create extra complexity, including opportunities for tax avoidance and evasion. Depending on the form of such taxation, rules pertaining to international transactions and financial institutions, among other areas, could remain complicated.

Summary

The enormous tax gap exerts a progressively debilitating impact on the fairness and productivity of the tax system. A poorly-functioning tax system impedes economic efficiency and growth. Perceived injustices of the system sap confidence and weaken the public resolve to play by the rules. And now especially, in light of serious deficit problems, upgrading tax enforcement is not only important for the health of the U.S. economy, but it is an urgent priority in fiscal policy. A variety of remedies have been found to provide very high revenue payoffs over and above very modest costs.

There are few free lunches in economics. Better tax enforcement may not be free, but it is one of the best bargains available in economic policy.

Endnote

1.   Because this chapter aims to provide a non-technical overview of the topic, citations have been kept to a minimum. Data on the tax gap are from the IRS (2005). The benefit/cost ratios of assorted enforcement measures are from Plumley (1996; 2004). Information on the IRS workload, audit rates, and funding is from Rossotti (2004), Burman (2004), and the IRS (2005). Some of the most recent research on tax enforcement can be found in Aaron and Slemrod (2004).

References

Aaron, Henry J. and Harvey Galper. 1985. *Assessing Tax Reform*. Washington, D.C.: The Brookings Institution.

Aaron, Henry J. and Joel Slemrod (eds). 2004. *The Crisis in Tax Administration*. Washington, D.C.: The Brookings Institution.

Burman, Leonard E. 2004. "On Waste, Fraud, and Abuse in Federal Mandatory Programs." Statement before the Committee on the Budget, United States House of Representatives. July 9.

Cherry, Robert and Max B. Sawicky. 2000. *Giving tax credit where credit is due: A 'universal unified child credit' that expands the EITC and cuts taxes for working families*. Briefing Paper #91. Washington, D.C.: Economic Policy Institute.

Dodge, Joseph M. and Jay A. Soled. 2005. "Inflated Tax Basis and the Quarter-Trillion-Dollar Revenue Question." *Tax Notes*, Vol. 106, No. 4, pp. 453-61.

Donmoyer, Ryan J. 2000. "Secret GAO Report Is Latest to Discredit Roth's IRS Hearings." *Tax Notes*, Volume 87, Number 4, p. 463-65.

Gale, William G. 2001. "Testimony Before the Subcommittee on Oversight and Subcommittee Select Revenue Measures of the House Committee on Ways and Means." Hearing Series on Tax Code Simplification. July 17.

Internal Revenue Service. 2005. "The Tax Gap." http://www.irs.gov/pub/irs-utl/tax_gap_facts-figures.pdf.

Johnston, David Cay. 2003. *Perfectly Legal: The Covert Campaign to Rig Our Tax System to Benefit the Super Rich—and Cheat Everybody Else*. New York, N.Y.: Portfolio.

Kenney, Allen. 2005a. "Everson Evaluates State of IRS, Pledges Strong Agenda for 2005." *Tax Notes*, Vol. 106, No. 1, pp. 40-44.

Kenney, Allen. 2005b. "Oversight Board Wants Bigger IRS Budget in 2006 Than Bush, Everson." *Tax Notes*, Vol. 106, No. 12, p. 1348-50.

Kenney, Allen. 2005c. "IRS to Reopen Debt Collection Contract Bidding." *Tax Notes*, Vol. 108, No. 7, p. 628.

Maag, Elaine. 2005. "Disparities in Knowledge of the EITC." *Tax Notes*, Vol. 106, No. 11, p. 1323.

Plumley, Alan. 1996. *The Determinants of Individual Income Tax Compliance: Estimating the Impacts of Tax Policy, Enforcement, and IRS Responsiveness*. Department of the Treasury, Internal Revenue Service.

Plumley, Alan. 2004. "Overview of the Federal Tax Gap." Department of the Treasury, Internal Revenue Service, NHQ Office of Research.

Price, Lee and Max B. Sawicky. 2004. *The budget arithmetic test: Repairing federal fiscal policy*. Briefing Paper #153. Washington, D.C.: Economic Policy Institute.

Rossotti, Charles O. 2002. "Report to the IRS Oversight Board: Assessment of the IRS and the Tax System." http://www.irsoversightboard.treas.gov/documents/commissioner_report.pdf.

Rossotti, Charles O. 2004. Letter to Senators Charles Grassley and Max Baucus.

Sawicky, Max B. 2002. *Where the money isn't: Misplaced focus of tax enforcement could be remedied by simplifying credits for children.* Issue Brief #183. Washington, D.C.: Economic Policy Institute.

Sawicky, Max B. 2005. *Collision course: The Bush budget and Social Security.* Briefing Paper # 156. Washington, D.C.: Economic Policy Institute.

Scott, Cordia. 2004. "OECD Targets More Financial Centers in Tax Haven Crackdown." *Tax Notes,* Vol. 103, No. 11, pp. 1347-49.

Slemrod, Joel. 2004. "Does the Tax System Penalize, or Favor, Small Business?" *The Crisis in Tax Administration.* Aaron and Slemrod, eds. Washington, D.C.: The Brookings Institution.

Steuerle, C. Eugene. 1998. "Pension and Saving Incentives by the Bushel-Load." *Tax Notes.* Vol. 79, p. 1769.

Stratton, Sheryl. 2005. "Officials Gauge Government Success in War on Shelters." *Tax Notes,* Vol. 106, No. 8, pp. 883-84.

Sullivan, Martin A. 2004. "U.S. Citizens Hide Hundreds of Billions in Cayman Accounts." *Tax Notes,* Vol. 103, No. 8, pp. 956-64.

Survey of Current Business. 2004. Table 1, p. 11. November.

Tax Notes. 2001. "Deal Letter to Treasury Opposing OECD Info Exchange Initiative." p. 1269. December 3.

Transactional Records Access Clearinghouse (TRAC). 2005. "TRAC/IRS: National Profile and Enforcement Trends over Time." http://trac.syr.edu/tracirs/newfindings/current/#figure5.

Wasow, Bernard. 2002. *Earned Income Credit: The Compliance Challenge.* Issue Brief. Washington, D.C.: The Century Foundation.

Williams, David C. 2000. "Progress and Problems in Implementing the Internal Revenue Service Restructuring and Reform Act of 1998." Statement for the record by the Treasury Inspector General for Tax Administration, joint hearing before committees of the United States Senate and House of Representatives. May 3.

CHAPTER 2

Interview: Sheldon S. Cohen

*Max B. Sawicky interviews Sheldon Cohen, former commis-
sioner of the Internal Revenue Service during the administration
of President Lyndon B. Johnson.*

Please tell us a bit about your background before joining the IRS.

I have to start with the United States Navy. When I enlisted in the U.S.
Navy in the spring of 1945 at the age of 17, I was to be an electronic
technician—a radar technician. But the war ended while I was in training, and they gave me two choices. The Navy said I could either enlist for
two years or I could either be a secretary or a bookkeeper in a separation
center. They told me, "That's what we need now; we don't need the things
we were training you for, unless you're going to stay in the Navy."

I said okay, I'll be a bookkeeper. I originally wanted to be an elec-
trical engineer and bookkeeping would be a way to keep my mathemati-
cal skills up. I went off to bookkeeping school and I had the misfortune
of graduating first in the class, but it drove me crazy because nobody
ever told me *why* I was doing anything. The Navy taught bookkeeping
by rote: they only told me what to do.

After that, I enrolled in Armed Forces training programs in accounting. That was how I got into accounting. When I got out of the Navy,
instead of going to engineering school I went to accounting school. As
a senior in accounting school, I thought maybe I ought to get a law
degree, because it would help my accounting, not because I wanted to
be a lawyer.

When I finished law school, I was offered a teaching fellowship,
and I had a couple of job offers. I went to see one of my professors for
advice. He said to me, if you're going to practice tax law, go practice
tax law. Don't teach or do all these other things. So I went to the

21

IRS. I didn't know enough about the law to know what I wanted because no one in my family had ever gone to college, much less professional school.

I was talking to the top person there. The chief counsel asked me, where would you like to work? I said, I don't know about the organization. I want to do the things you think I'll do the best, where I'll do the best. He put me in legislative drafting.

What year was this?

This is 1952. It ended up that I was the youngest of the group that drafted the 1954 Code when it was enacted. There were about 12 or 15 of us, and a few supervisors. That's how I got into the tax field and went to work for the IRS. I worked at the IRS for a little over four years, from 1952 to 1956. Then I left and went to work for the law firm Paul, Weiss for a few years and then Arnold, Fortas, and Porter after that. When I came back to the IRS, Lyndon Johnson appointed me chief counsel and later commissioner within a few weeks, three or four weeks almost to the day after the assassination of Kennedy.

Scrutiny

Let's start with a broad question. What do you think are the chief problems right now in tax enforcement, and what are the most likely remedies? How would you lay those out in summary?

We have no tax enforcement, basically. We are auditing something on the order of six tenths of one percent of returns. There is also computer checking. That is, when you send in a return, it's automatically checked for math accuracy. You can't file a return with arithmetic errors because the machine won't take it; it will correct it. We get that kind of supervision, but we've had that since my day. When I was commissioner, we put most of those systems in.

In the beginning, we didn't check every return for math accuracy; we checked most of them. By the time I left in 1969, we were checking them all. From 1969 to today, you're doing it faster, the computers are quicker. We used to do it on Univac computers that would take two, three rooms.

But the scrutiny is another thing altogether. If I'm a business-man and I'm chiseling a little bit, I don't have to fear that a revenue agent is going to come look over my shoulder and say this looks wrong. It happens so rarely that it's now being discounted, and people therefore become more and more brazen. Gresham's Law applies in social science as well as economics: bad practice drives out good.

We get these tax shelter kinds of things, and we get tax protester movements that flourish because there's just not enough enforcement. If everybody knew someone who was audited—that there is some check-ing—then we would all behave. That doesn't mean that there have to be substantial changes. We behave on a highway when we see a traffic policeman every once in a while. We need to see the traffic policeman every once in a while to stay relatively close to the law.

The shelter problem has been discussed a lot. How big is the protester problem?

Too big. One is too many; hundreds are much too many. We're talking about thousands.

Thousands?

Yes, not hundreds of thousands. One begets another. The Service just saw a case a couple of weeks ago with a former IRS special agent who is now a tax protester, a guy named Bannister. The jury thought he had an excuse in wanting to file a protest return, if you will, so he was acquitted. This is a special agent who was charged with en-forcing the law for many years and shortly after he leaves, he files one of these cockamamie protest returns saying that the income tax was not properly ratified.

The tax legislation?

Yes. There's a group of protesters running around the country who say that the 16th Amendment was never properly ratified. That's one of their excuses.

Why couldn't everybody do that?

That gets you off the criminal charge. It doesn't get you off the tax, because it is not true.

He's still liable for the tax.

Yes, and you need to go out and find those people and find them as quickly as possible and bring them in, and collect the tax, so that their brothers and their sisters and their friends don't get the idea that they can try this. Because it doesn't work. The only way to convince them of that is to audit enough of them.

You say we have no enforcement. Where should the priority be right now in terms of escalation?

You have the terrible problem that the administration's greatest political strength is in small business. That's also where you have the largest non-compliance. My father's favorite joke illustrates the point. Forgive me for telling a joke. It's about a man who walks into the dry cleaners. He puts down his dry cleaning ticket, and the owner brings him a suit of clothes. He puts down a bill, and the owner gives him change for a twenty dollar bill. As the man is walking out of the store, the owner looks down and sees, as he's putting the money in the cash register, that he was handed a fifty, not a twenty.

He's struck with a moral dilemma: does he tell his partner? That's the joke. You've got to look at people, you have to check, because if left to their own devices, they'll say, "If I can't get caught, why shouldn't I do it? Why shouldn't I take this deduction?"

One of the terrible things I had to do was send Audie Murphy to jail. Audie Murphy was the most decorated soldier in World War II. He made up charitable deductions and just plugged them into his return. It was just awful. The judge was lenient on him because of who he was. If you don't catch those kinds of people, they will take advantage. The worst part of it is that it feeds on itself, because if you don't catch the first one, he tells five others, and soon those five are doing it too.

The small business crowd steals, not because they're worse morally than anybody else, but because they have the opportunity. Mom and pop are running the business, and they have access to the cash register and to the other records. They can do it without the participation of a lot of people. I've often told developing countries, "You'll be safe when business gets bigger and mom and pop can't control the business anymore." They need more people to help them run the business. They have to build systems to protect themselves against those people. They protect the government at the same time, when they build those protective systems.

What's the most productive way to remedy the small business problem?

More audits.

Just more audits?

Small businesses are so varied; you can't have a cookie-cutter solution. You've got a small consultant firm that does economic consulting, and you've got one that does accounting, and you've got one that does law, and you've got one that runs a grocery store, and one that runs a sewing shop. Each one has a different problem. It's like saying you could have one universal accounting system that will work for everybody. You can't, because the systems are too varied.

The audit rate now is under 1%.

The last time I looked, it was about six tenths of a percent.

Off the top of your head, if you could set a small business audit rate that would create enough of a ripple effect, where would you set it? What would you shoot for?

Two and a half, 3%. If it were 4.5%, it would be too labor-intensive, but you'd have much better compliance. Before I left, we had fully operational computer systems, but in 1964 and 1965 we were just beginning. By 1966 and 1967 it was pretty much in, and by 1969 when I left it was operational.

We don't have the full results out of the National Research Project (NRP) that's ongoing right now. That's going to help somewhat, but the project worries me because the samples are so shallow. I'm not enough of a statistician to know how valid their samples are.

Would the same focus be appropriate for S-corporations and part-nerships?

Sure.

It's all similar?

When you talk about the thousand biggest corporations in America, we're auditing a very heavy percentage of those. We audit those probably on the order of every year. If you go to the next several thousand, it's once every two or three years. It falls off after that. When you get out of the first several thousand, the numbers start going down dramatically. There is more opportunity to steal, and therefore more stealing. It isn't that these people are more evil than other people; they aren't. They just have more opportunity.

The politics of tax enforcement legislation

We used to have enforcement, but now we have no enforcement. How did this unfold?

There's always a dynamic tension. There are people in Congress who want you to enforce the law, but not against their constituents or against the groups that they favor. You deal with two sets of people when you're commissioner. You deal with the one set of people who are the sub-stance people, the people on the Ways and Means Committee. They are interested in the substance of the tax law, and a little less interested in administration, interestingly enough, although once in a while you get somebody who becomes interested in administration. J.J. Pickle, former chairman of the House Subcommittee on Oversight of the Ways and Means Committee, was interested in substance, but recently we haven't had anyone who was actively interested in the oversight committees, which are not very active these days.

Then there are the people on the appropriations committees. The problem is that they look at the IRS as though it were a spending agency. They ask, "We're giving you two billion dollars, or four billion dollars." It's up to 10 or 11 now. "How are you spending it?" They don't spend nearly as much time asking, "How much are you raising with it? What's your multiple?"

We always said we needed more people, interestingly enough, even when I was there. When I was there, we ran with maybe 65,000 people during the height of the filing season. Today, they have close to 95,000. It used to be 110,000. They're down by at least 15,000 or 20,000 people, over their peak period, from three or four years ago.

I became commissioner in 1965. It's been 40 years since I was appointed. In that period of time, the population has probably grown nearly 100%. The population has close to doubled in that period of time. It usually goes up on the order of 2% a year, either by birth or immigration.

We had a rule of thumb. We would not ask for money unless we could bring in at least six times what we were asking for. It was usually on the order of 10 to 12 times.

Were you able to document the output?

Usually. We moved from filing in the 66 or 67 or 68 districts to filing in seven service centers. There was a lead time to see the efficacy of it, but you can imagine the efficiency that was gained, relatively quickly, after the break-in period.

In terms of the politics, was there any counterpart then to what looks today like a political constituency that really doesn't want the government to function well? Was there anything like that then, or was it different?

It was much smaller, and much less powerful, and there was a much harder argument for them to make than they seem to make now. That doesn't mean there weren't conservatives who thought the government ought to be less intrusive, and that the income tax was too high or unconstitutional. Those arguments were made then, but they were not taken so seriously, nor was there so much respectability in making them.

I could be looking at it through rose-colored glasses, but when I think of somebody like Barry Goldwater, I think of somebody who certainly wanted smaller government and lower taxes, but not someone promoting measures that would sabotage the functioning of government.

The liberals and the conservatives dealt with each other as human beings and as people, and not as the enemy. They didn't take it nearly so personally. They could be yelling at each other on the floor, and taking each other to dinner at night.

When I was in the office, Alcohol, Tobacco, and Firearms was part of the IRS. Once I was testifying in favor of gun control, gun restrictions on importation, which eventually became the Firearms Control Act of 1968. Senator Roman Hruska was yelling and screaming at me. I was before the Senate, I think the Judiciary Committee. He was just tearing me apart. During one of the breaks he walked over, looked at me, and said, "Sheldon, don't worry, I'm doing this for the folks back home." He was nice enough to tell me it was not personal, which made it a little easier, though I still had to take the garbage coming at me. I don't think they do that today; they'll go through the charade but they won't tell you it's for fun.

They really mean it this time.

Yes, that's true for either side. The liberals and the conservatives are equally guilty of that sort of thing. Everything becomes personalized. I mean, these jobs are terrible and hard to do anyway, and when you have to take this personal grief, it doesn't make it any easier.

Maybe the change in the balance of power makes the winners insecure and suspicious and the losers bitter and resentful; if they were to establish an eternal order, I guess people would also get along with each other better.

That's as good an analysis as any. You also have the techniques for gerrymandering and setting up districts that made the liberals more liberal and the conservatives more conservative, and there are fewer people in the middle.

The taxpayer as customer

There's been criticism of a shift from enforcement to what commissioners Fred Goldberg and Charles Rossotti would talk about as service. The taxpayer is the customer.

The taxpayer is not a customer. You didn't choose him and he didn't choose you. In a customer situation, I choose which department store I want to go into, and they choose to have me as a paying customer or not. In the situation we have in the tax system, the revenue service collects the tax. They're mandated to do it, and the taxpayer has no choice but to comply. The analogy is a bad analogy. On the other hand, the taxpayer ought to be treated with respect and courtesy.

Cohen's rule was that you don't have to agree with me, but you shouldn't be disagreeable about it. That is, you ought to have their respect. That doesn't mean they'll like you. You're not going to make them like you. You are requiring somebody to pay a tax. Often he doesn't want to pay; often it's more than he thinks is fair. I mean, it's not his judgment, nor is it yours. Congress made the judgment as to what the amount is for certain ranges. You're dealing with a system that has inherent tensions in it. You can't get away from them. All you can do is to say to your people, "Be respectful of the taxpayer. Be respectful of their rights. Explain them, but don't back off." I don't think you can treat them as a customer, because the customer is always right, my father told me. My father was in the wholesale food business, and the customer was always right. Even when he was wrong, he was right, because he's the customer, he's the boss.

The taxpayer is not your boss. He's not the one who wrote the law. The Congress wrote the law. The law doesn't always work fairly, but it's the law nevertheless. You swear an oath of office to enforce the law, not to enforce your version of the law.

Taking all that as given, could the IRS be doing more in the realm of service and education, profitably?

It should. For example—and this used to be done pretty extensively for a long time, though it's not done nearly as much now—we had a course that we would provide free to every high school system in the United States that would be part of a civics or a math course and would teach people about the tax system. It would be three or four lessons in which they would learn enough about the tax system and the rudimentary nature of it. Students would get an understanding of the tax system so that when they went out into the real world later on, they would have some knowledge about it. That kind of training is important, but it's hard to get anybody's attention for that kind of stuff anymore.

Privatization of tax collection

Since you bring that up, there is the administration's interest in contracting out some collections. What do you think the prospects for that being effective are?

The problem with that is that we have entirely different sets of rules for those people than we do have for IRS people. That is, IRS people, by law, may not be judged for promotion on the basis of what they collect or what they assess. We know that people in private industry are going to be judged on the basis of what they collect.

How much money they're bringing in?

Yes, how much money they bring in—that's the whole purpose of bidding on this contract. We have two sets of rules. The IRS will have all the hard cases, because these contractors are not going to be allowed to get into the intricacies of tax returns. They're only going to be around to deal with accepted liability. If there are any questions or problems with returns or with taxpayer's understanding of the liability, those immediately fall back to the IRS. All the hard cases fall to the IRS. All the easy cases are going to be handled by people in private industry. I'm not sure what you'll get out of it.

If they're easy, would it be a good deal for the government?

If they're easy, yes. The interesting thing is that on the data I have seen, and that's the data from the present Internal Revenue Service's management system, if you took the same dollars that you were to pay these private collectors and hired collection officers, we'd collect more money. The problem is that the Congress has some kind of ceiling that won't allow the IRS to have more than a certain number of people. If you have an artificial ceiling on personnel, the only way you can get more people is to contract out. It really is kind of silly.

When I was talking to (former commissioner) Donald Alexander, he suggested that there was a very high fixed cost of getting into the business, so it really wasn't economical to duplicate that fixed cost in the private sector in order to chase these collections.

I don't know that there is or there isn't. There are private bill collectors and they have a lot of the systems set up. Now what additional systems or controls the IRS may require of them, I don't know. I mean I don't look at the contract closely enough to be able to discern that the entry costs would be that high.

How would the contract employees be related to the so-called "10 Deadly Sins"?[1]

That is the problem.

Could they commit any of those sins?

They will, you know they will. The problem is: how are they going to be supervised, and how carefully are the private supervisors going to enforce those restrictions? When somebody complains and it goes to the IRS and the IRS Inspector General, and the Treasury Inspector General takes a look, you'll have a report, three years, five years from now saying that the private contractors committed these seven of the 10 deadly sins or whatever the number it is, and in larger or smaller percentages than collection officers do. Larger, I suspect, but we don't know that because it hasn't happened yet. We do know that two or three experiments like this have occurred over the last number of years, and there have been no good results out of it. Each of the test runs that have been done to do something like this has not worked. They didn't bring in greater dollars.

There was no dividend.

There was no bonus here. If you had given the same money to the service, the service would have brought you more money.

Will the contractors in this business be paid according to how many dollars they bring in?

They're basically going to be paid on, I think, 25% of what they bring in. The Congress pretends that's new money.

It wouldn't make the IRS work that way.

No, no. The IRS was once given a circular fund like that, and we kept bringing in more. We never used up the fund. There was always money in it. But Congress just doesn't like to see more federal employees, and they treat an IRS employee exactly like somebody who is at Housing and Urban Development or Health and Human Services handing out subsidies. They treat them the same. They're not the same: one is bringing in 10 times his salary, or maybe a little more, and the other is spending money, and that's his function, to spend money.

It sounds like Congress wants to put limits on how well the IRS does its job, despite all their rhetoric.

Exactly. I was lucky—I lived in a time when people believed in a performance budget. That is, you submitted your budget, and if you brought in what you said you'd bring in, you got more money.

They talk about doing that all the time now.

But they don't do it.

There's a gigantic campaign....

That was Bob McNamara's theory, it was the second Hoover Commission's. The second Hoover Commission believed in using those kinds of incentives in government, and they worked. We got more money, and we did a better job. That's not to say it didn't whack us once in awhile; it did. In a political climate, if somebody in the opposition has a fix on a particular industry, they'll come try to clip you, saying that you shouldn't audit this industry or that industry. We had problems with fish farms. They're still having problems with fish farms, as I understand it.

Fish farms?

Yes, fish farms. You build ponds, you raise fish, and you sell fish. It's like any other small business; there are a gazillion ways that you can chisel in on those things. Should you audit more of them, or should you audit less of them? It's the usual dynamic. If you look at the Internal Revenue Code, it's full of all kinds of benefits for farmers. We used to joke that whatever the rule was, it was 10% less for farmers. That was just a house joke, but it's true. Congress will put in a special benefit for farmers. They have to pay less of an estimated tax than somebody else does. The penalties are less, the allowances are greater.

Mysteries of accounting

Shouldn't the profit companies report to their shareholders be the same as the profit they report to the IRS?

Yes. This is a problem that goes all the way back. I've been practicing tax law for 53 years. It goes back to the beginning. I mean, I teach a course at George Washington University Law School called "Accounting for Lawyers." The problem is the exceptions. My accountant friends will take great umbrage at what I'm going to say, but one of the problems was that until recently—and including recently—the ethics of both the law and the accounting profession were not what they should have been. There were always some practitioners who were shifting the edges. In fact, in the 1954 Code, there was an attempt (and I was the person who made the attempt; I was the draftsman of Section 452 and 462) to try to get book and accounting for accounting purposes and accounting for tax purposes closer together. We had estimated expenses and we had pre-

paid income, those were the two big deviations, and we tried to get
it closer together. We kept warning our superiors at Treasury that
the accounting profession did not have good definitions in these
things, and what would happen is they'd start changing the definitions if we changed the code.

Good definitions or different definitions?

They would slide the definitions to fit the code. We enacted provisions to allow them to defer prepaid income. If somebody pays for
a three-year magazine subscription in December, it runs for three
years. If you buy it in December, you only have one month this
year, you've got all the next year, all the following year and a piece
of the third year. You could defer that. That's prepaid income because the magazine gets that money right away.

Also, you've got estimated expenses. An airplane is allowed to
fly 1,000 hours, say, before it has to be overhauled, so for every
hour it flies you have an estimated expense. Suppose it's going to
cost $10,000 to overhaul the engine. You have a charge per mile
that you could charge beforehand, so that at the end of the 1,000
hours, you've got the money to pay it.

*In both of those cases, shouldn't these things be charged when
they're either received or when the income and the outgo actually
happen?*

You've asked a question to which there is no good answer, because
accounting theory has been on all sides of that question, and *is* on
all sides. What we found, however, when I was a kid, is that the
accountants kept changing the definitions on us. The Securities
and Exchange Commission had no good rules then, and there was
no accounting oversight board then, which there is now. There are
still deviations, by the way.

But that's still a problem: who makes up accounting standards?
Who makes up the rules by which the accounting field judges itself? Now we do have a quasi-governmental organization, this accounting oversight board, reviewing standards, and the Securities
and Exchange Commission has a bigger role than it did in the past.
You could bring them closer together, but the problem is that the

urgency in the field for the results you want is different depending on whether it is reporting income for shareholder purposes or reporting income for tax purposes.

In principle, you want to tell a different story to a different audience.

You do, and the Congress has allowed it. There were members of Congress as recently as this summer who were trying to stop the accounting oversight board and the SEC from imposing tougher rules on the accounting profession. Look at the fight we are having right now about the expensing of stock options.[2] SEC chairman Christopher Cox was one of the persons who introduced a bill to block that particular change.

Who should be the czar that gives us the rules?

Interestingly enough, when I was in office, the leading public accountants were public policy types of the neutral sort, like Leonard Spacek (the head of Arthur Andersen, then the leader in this field). He had an idea, and I applauded it, of an accounting court: a special court that would adopt accounting rules. It's too much like the standard setting group that is quasi-governmental. But you see that every once in a while the issue is finessed by the Congress.

It's happened two or three times in the last three years, with the stock option issue. Every time we're about to issue it, Congress threatens it, so they back off, and they don't ever issue it. Here we have this anomaly that I pay my president partially by stock options, with publicly traded stock in a high-flying new industry. It shows up as an expense on the tax return, but it doesn't show up as an expense on the financial statements. Every time somebody tries to make that rule uniform, saying that it should show up on a financial statement, the Congress blocks it. We'll see what happens. It's been an ongoing problem the whole 50 years I've been practicing, getting a little better, but not much.

There were financial scandals in the 1930s that propelled the Roosevelt administration to some reforms. Did any of that hinge on accounting?

It's all better. It's all better than it was 50 years ago, 75 years ago. But it's only marginally better. This accounting oversight board is going to bring some more attention to it. The accounting standards board is doing a better job, and it's got a little more guts than it used to have, but it still backs off quite often. It gets threatened by a chairman of a major committee, and they back off.

Is a consumption tax easy to administer?

One of the controversies in tax reform hinges on the intrinsic diffi-culties of measuring income that, in some people's view, points to the marriage of some kind of cash-flow income tax that potentially facilitates enforcement.

It wouldn't facilitate enforcement. The problem is that you can control your cash flow. You may get rich as hell because everybody says you're rich. Money is that which people treasure. If you're doing a great job and you're making lots of money in the abstract sense, people are going to value your business nevertheless, so they have a stock value that be-lies what you're reporting, because you aren't reporting anything.

In a cash-flow framework, that would be taxable when you sold an interest and therefore you had some market transactions.

Suppose I don't sell? Suppose I'm Bill Gates and I don't have to sell?

Then there's no tax yet.

Exactly, and there's Bill Gates, who is a very rich man—and he should be because he's done a remarkable job—but he pays no tax, and the guy who's driving the garbage truck does pay tax. I find that a little hard to deal with, and I think a lot of other people do too. The problem is you always have that guy who is driving the garbage truck, and he's easy to deal with.

In principle, you can have graduated rates to compensate for a switch from income to consumption and eventually nail Bill Gates.

There is no 'eventually.' The United States' budget is built day-by-day. If you allow me to defer my income in some way, and allow yourself to defer it tomorrow, and a third guy to defer it the next day, and a fourth guy to defer it the following day, the United States never collects that money. It's a continuum. Most people don't understand that a dollar's worth of tax deferred, in the context of the IRS, is a dollar's worth of tax never collected, because there's a continuum. It's always somebody.

All of us with 401K's, when we pull our money out, we're going to pay tax on that, right?

Maybe not. Maybe yes, maybe no. I've seen too many exceptions put in there lately. It's hardship. I die and it goes on to my kids, my grandkids, onward and upward.

We were talking with Donald Alexander about the estate tax for family corporations....

There's a lot of argument, for example, that the estate tax is a double tax. The truth of the matter is that most of what the estate tax reaches has never been taxed: all appreciated real estate, all appreciated securities, deferred compensation. All those things have never been reached, never been taxed. Nor has the benefit of deferral all that time been taxed. We don't have a cruel tax in that sense, and there are a variety of reasons that we don't have it. The interesting thing is that, if we go to carryover basis[3], then it makes it worse for most people. Most people would be worse off with a carryover basis.

As things stand, the rules allow this appreciation, this accumulated income, to be shielded from tax indefinitely if the asset is never sold through family corporations.

And with dynasty trusts.

Dynasty trusts: how do those work?

I'm not really a great expert. The problem is that, if I can defer a dollar for 20 years, then it becomes three dollars, or five dollars, because of the accrual during that period of time. Even if you tax me at full rates when I realize, the United States is never even. If we taxed it when it was earned, we would have had that money, and the United States would have had the accrual. You're chasing your tail; you never catch up that way.

The carryover basis is tied up with the repeal of the estate tax.

Bob Dole got that passed in the 1980s, as I remember it. I think I was the only one who testified, when he sponsored the carryover basis. Then he got beaten back because it never became effective. It was repealed.

There was a paper by Joel Slemrod and Bill Gale[4] that talked about this. They wrote that when carryover basis was enacted, it was thought to be unadministrable. Therefore it was dumped, and including it in the new legislation is basically a ruse. It will fall out of the law again.

Senator Bob Dole put it in and I was the only one who testified in favor of it. Carter was president, so it was in the late 1970s. Somebody in the Carter Administration asked me if I would testify. The theory was: if a guy sold an asset 15 minutes before he died, he would need to know the basis of the asset. Why? What's the difference if his executors sell it 15 minutes after he dies? It might be hard; it's worse if you go three generations. If you get carryover basis and you go two or three generations, you'll be worse off.

Will the IRS be able to administer that, assuming it stays in the law?

No. The only way the IRS will administer it is if you don't put the basis in; basis will be zero.

...then a higher tax burden falls on the taxpayer.

Sure the burden's on the taxpayer. I know the basis of my house. I've lived in that house for more than 40 years, and I have kept a tally sheet on every improvement that I've made for the house. It may not be exact, but it's close. If we took out the old windows, I knew what the bill for the new ones was. I didn't know what the old ones cost that we took out. Nobody else does it because it isn't necessary in the present system. For most people, if they died with that house, it would have a fair market value the day of their death. With carryover basis and with adjustments and exchanges that we've had, we could always bury all those problems.

Those problems would come to the fore with the present law that repeals the estate tax law in 2010 and reinstates it in 2011; there's the carryover basis. That's one of the corollaries. They did that because of the cost savings. They didn't do it out of the goodness of their heart or because they wanted to raise taxes, because that was a tax-cutting group that did it.

Social programs in the tax code ("tax expenditures")

With the proliferation of tax expenditures, there's a growing administrative burden. It strikes me as different in form from things that are technically complicated like transfer pricing or depreciation or valuing financial assets. Do you see it that way, or is it all more or less uniformly burdensome for the IRS?

The tax expenditures have gotten worse because of the pay-go's[5]. In the pay-go world, it was easier to enact a tax break for social purposes than it was to make an expenditure and have it go through all kinds of justifications. Not to collect the tax was a much easier thing to explain. There were also fewer committees to deal with. When you make an expenditure, you have to go through two committees in both houses. First, you have to go through the Authorizing Committee, which authorizes the expenditure, and then through the Appropriations Committee, which puts up the money. They often differ quite dramatically. They'll authorize a zillion bucks and then only pay half a zillion bucks or a quarter of a zillion bucks—whatever the number.

A tax break is a lot easier, because you don't need all those bodies to agree. Here you just have a Ways and Means and a Finance Committee and they agreed not to collect the tax from Sawicky and to collect the tax from Cohen, by defining us in whatever ways they define us. That's easier to do than pay-go, and once the Congress realized that, it obviated a lot of problems. It's a whole lot easier to deal with two committees than four. A larger body is much more difficult. Once the genie is out of the bottle and everybody knows how to do it, then they begin to do it.

It's catchy, and as you point out, it puts all the administrative burden on the revenue service instead of on the Agriculture Department or the Housing Department or the Welfare Department, where it ought to be. Who is administering the largest welfare program in the United States?[6] The Internal Revenue Service. Are they set up to do it? Of course not. Do they do it well? Of course not. But they do it.

During World War II and the Korean War, when we used to enact subsidies to get somebody to do something for the war effort, we said, "The Defense Mobilization Act of the agency shall certify that so-and-so is entitled to such-and-such," and give them money. Now we say he gets a tax credit, or a tax deduction as the case may be. It's a deviation from standard accounting, it's a deviation from all the other rules that apply to every other industry, and it makes for long tax returns because they all have to be explained. People ask, "Why don't you have a simple tax return for us simple folks, and let the complicated people have complicated tax returns?"

The IRS doesn't know who is who, and they aren't necessarily who they were last year. Mike Graetz's system[7] for taxing people who make more than $100,000 one way and less than $100,000 another way won't work, not because it isn't a nice system and he hasn't thought through a lot of the problems; he has. But there is no discipline when you don't know whether you have to file a tax return or not. If you make only $99,000 dollars, you don't file a return; if you make a $101,000, you do file a return. How do we teach the people from one year to the next?

You do the same work either way. You either pay or you don't.

I'm just pointing out the anomalies here. Greatz thinks there is a nice, sharp line between those who make $100,000 and those who don't. The problem is that people are jumping in and out of that bracket all the time. It's a lot more complicated than what Greenstein and Lav said in their article.[8]

Reorganizing the IRS

One of the watersheds in reorganizing the IRS was the Revenue Reform Act of 1998. How would you characterize the impact on enforcement?

It was devastating. The problem, of course, is that we found two or three years after the devastating set of hearings that most of the horror stories were not true; they were only partially true. The Congress reacted to a set of overblown problems, most of which did not exist or existed in a lesser form. Most of us who knew something about the tax knew that, but the Congress didn't convince itself until three or four years later.

If you were in a private corporation, you would evaluate a reorganization in terms of how much money it could save and how soon. If it couldn't recoup the cost of the changes within three to five years, it is unlikely that any major corporation would change its management system dramatically. It might change pieces of it, but it wouldn't change the whole system. There's no way in God's world the revenue service would get back anything like the money it has spent on reorganization over the past five or six years.

That act wasn't motivated by revenues. Ostensibly it was motivated by concern for people's rights.

But it turned out that people's rights weren't abused in the way that the accusations had stated. The principal accusers turned out to have given false statements or partially false statements. We've reorganized a whole system along particular business lines, depending on instant communication, when there is no instant communication. They use business-style techniques that rely on the ability to instantly communicate. The IRS has no fast response. It just isn't built that way. The revenue service was built in decentralized fashion on purpose, so that no one person could affect a decision involving any other person. That is how it was set up in 1952. I was there in 1952, and I helped draft some of those things.

How did the reorganization change that? It centralized?

It centralized. The control was centralized in a few hands.

To protect individual rights.

It was supposed to be more efficient. The commissioner was the only person in the revenue service who had direct line authority over anybody in the field when I was commissioner. I will tell you that I never once had anybody refuse to take a suggestion that I made. I never issued an order. I always said, "Why don't we do ..."

You were in charge.

No one ever said "Screw that, we ain't gonna do that," but that was because the staff trusted me, and they would have broken down any wall to do anything I asked them to do. Sometimes I was shocked at what they would do. But you had the protection of nobody. You have to remember that back in the 1950s there was a scandal in which an assistant attorney general went to jail, the commissioner went to jail, the chief counsel was fired in disgrace, and the president's cabinet secretary went to jail for fixing taxes.

In today's IRS, three or four people hav the ability to fix, or to change any result. Are they going to do it? I don't think so, but Murphy's Law applies: if anything can go wrong it will. Somebody will do it, someday—not today, not tomorrow, maybe the next day. Nobody took that into account. What has happened before can happen again. That's what history is supposed to teach us. The problem is that the guys who drafted that statute never read history. Would I do it this way? No. Would I have changed it totally? No. Would I have changed it somewhat? Yes. Would I have made substantial changes? Yes, but gradually, because sharp changes make for disruption, and the more disruption there is, the less tax that's collected. That's what you've had over the past few years.

How would you reorganize the service now, given where it's come?

The problem is that you're halfway through the changes and you can't turn it around. You've got to make the system that they've designed work. It is too far down the pike to turn around.

Do you think now it's too centralized and it's organized inefficiently?

The thing is that now you have terrible problems just doing simple things. For instance, who has the corner office in the IRS building in Nashville? Who decides that? There used to be a district director in Nashville, and he ladled out the offices. He was on the spot. He knew the people and the functions. Who does it now? There isn't anybody in charge of that now.

Who is the spokesman for the revenue service in Nashville where there are five or six other functions? Who is the spokesman, when it comes to an issue that's a local issue, and not a national issue? There are a whole lot of problems like that and that's the reverse of what they're thinking about. But all those kinds of issues come up, will come up, and are coming up every day. Who's going to answer?

It's still in flux.

Yes, they get better at it as they go along.

Return-free tax systems

Assuming it was possible to offload a lot of tax expenditure programs to other departments, what would be the possibilities for a substantially return-free system?

We had a system in the 1950s (I think it was the 1950s) that was similar to return-free. If you worked at one job and got a W-2, if that was your only job and you had no more than a few hundred dollars in dividends or interest, you could turn that W-2 over, and it was a 1040A. Your income was already there. All you had to do was put in your interest and dividends, which you got on a 1099, and file it. That was your return.

The problem was: what if you have three jobs? People filed three returns, because each time a W-2 would come in, they'd fill it out and send it in. The revenue service now had three returns for Max Sawicky or Sheldon Cohen. That was why it failed. We still have that problem, that is, people's incomes are diverse and come from a variety of sources.

If we had a P-A-Y-E[9] system like they have in Britain—where they have very detailed reporting to their employer and it's very intrusive—and if people complied with that system, we could probably get close to a return-free system. The problem is that we don't have a computer system that's responsive enough to give you the information you need to file quickly. In time we might, but we don't have it yet. That isn't to say I can't conceive of one; I can conceive it.

Is it conceivable to have a parallel return-free system where people could opt for a much simpler tax process?

Dual systems are inherently complex. Here's an illustration. President Johnson said to me personally, looked me square in the face and said, "You've got to design a simple form. That's my number one priority. I hired Livigard Margolis, a design firm for private industry To design a new form. Every time they came in with a brilliant idea, we said, "You can't do that." They would ask, "Why?" "Because the statute doesn't let you." You can't change the statute. This form has to comply with the statute. Assuming we were starting with a clean slate, we designed a form which was like a typical questionnaire: name, address, do you have any dividend income? If the answer is no, skip to next section, if the answer is yes, fill it in. No addition, just fill in the numbers. The return was seven or eight pages long.

We tried it on 100 secretaries in the national office, reasonably intelligent people, but with no tax background, on the reasoning that if we gave it to tax people the results would be distorted. We got back a 70% favorable rating. We said, "Use your tax information from last year; just plug it in." Then we tried it on a larger sample and still got a very high response. The staff said, "Let's try it nationwide." I said no. I said, "I'm going to send this to a hundred million people I don't know, on the basis of a few hundred?"

People we tested said, "When you get to the end of the questionnaire, you don't know what you owe." We had to put in an option that provided tax rates and brackets. Fill in this form and that gives you the tax, but you don't *have* to fill it in.

How many returns came in uncomputed? Virtually none. Today, you can file a 1040A on the Internet, and the government will compute your tax. How many are filing that way? Hardly any, because when people get to the end, they want to know if they owe money or if they will get a refund. We said, "What the hell are we doing? We're doing all this work, and taxpayers are doing all the work for us anyway."

Assuming you had two different ways that you could file, and the statute allowed either way—you could choose—undoubtedly some people would do it both ways.

That's what we discovered from this test; in effect, they did it both ways. But it wasn't a total failure, because we learned something. We did good scientific research that told us that we weren't going to get any good results this way. Thank God I didn't try it on a hundred million people, because I'm pretty sure that our 1% was pretty representative.

IRS computer problems

You raised the topic of computers. What was the IRS's challenge in improving its computer system?

They're running a computer system right now that is mostly based on stuff I left there 40 years ago. Some of that stuff is written in Cobol, and for some of their programs, you've got to hire a retired person my age to maintain the code. The young computer experts don't know Cobol.

Some banks still run Cobol.

You can make a lot of money if you know Cobol. That was just one of the problems. They were dealing with such an old system that had been patched and patched and patched.

The guys I hired were out of the Defense Supply Agency, because they had computers and they had been using them a few years. They were light years ahead of us. IBM gave us the best service in the world because we were going to be there. If our system worked, then they would have great sales for banks and all the financial institutions, and that is what happened.

Why can't the IRS transition?   They tried.

They tried to leapfrog. Instead of getting a better system, they tried to get the best system and go several generations ahead, and they just couldn't make it. In other words, their aim was too high. The enemy of better is best. They wanted the best system in the world, and they tried too hard. That's the Cohen analysis.

They're back to an antique mode of operation.

Yes. They should just make it better. When we put in the system, we couldn't send all that data over the wire. We were afraid to anyway because of the security problems. I think you still have those kinds of security problems.

Worse than ever, apparently.

Oh, you can imagine: leaks of the basic tax information.

Conclusion

How would you summarize the main priorities for the service?   Which would be the main things to focus on?

The main problem that caused the second 1998 act was the computer. If you go back to the hearings before the Commission that made the recommendations, it was all about the computer: that the computer was antiquated and inadequate and had to be modernized. There was less worry about centralization. They hardly addressed the central problem. They're only creeping up on it now.

The technology?

Yes, the technology. That reflects badly on (former commissioner) Charles Rossotti, I'm afraid. Charles was hired because he was a computer person, not because he knew anything about the tax system. He didn't profess to know about it. From conception to installation, it took about seven or eight years for the IRS to put the first computer system in. Seven or eight years wouldn't be bad, but they've used up the first seven years already.

How would better technology facilitate enforcement?

If you contact a collection officer because you can't reconcile your tax bill with your records, the officer has a hard time calling up your records on disk, unless it was already assigned to him and he had it on his desk. If you contact Chase Manhattan Bank or any of the major credit card companies, they'll call up your records fairly quickly and efficiently. Of course, a bank account is a lot less complex.

Originally the IRS was a completely decentralized system. There were seven service centers that had the full records, and one national center. The seven sent summaries of their takes to the national center, so you had a national take. If you can't call up the record, you can't answer taxpayers' problem when they call you on the telephone. Of course, in this modern day and age, you can't ever get the same person you called. You go through the same story five times, because it's a different person who answers the telephone each time.

That's a service problem. What about enforcement?

That's a big service problem. On the enforcement side, they just don't have the personnel. When you move from 120,000 people to 95,000 or whatever it is now, the first person you cut is not an administrative or filing person.

It's not the people who must process returns.

It is a collection officer or a revenue agent, because that's your only margin of flexibility. You've got to process returns. You've got to do all the accounting work. None of that is elective. The only elective things you've got to do are collect and audit. Nobody was thinking about the fact that dramatic personnel cuts were going to fall disproportionately on enforcement or that the cuts might have a deleterious effect on people's behavior, and it has. We went through that at the same time society was just becoming less and less compliant. People are more and more maverick.

In light of the picture you painted, it seems almost miraculous that they collect as much as they do.

Yes, yes. The system by and large still works. It's falling apart on the edges and it gets worse and harder. The more deterioration there is, the harder it is going to be to bring it back. I don't belittle that. On the other hand, when you compare it to most systems in the world, it still works pretty well. Where we are doing terribly, the hole in the income tax (the "tax gap" the share of taxes owed that is not paid voluntarily and on time) is about 15%. What's the failure to collect the Value Added Tax (VAT) in Britain? It's over 16%. The VAT is supposed to be easier to collect than the income tax, but I don't believe it.

The point is, in spite of all those problems we're still doing pretty well. You can't look at it in isolation. You've got to compare it to something else, and compared to something else, we're doing pretty well. Now the American people are fairly compliant; most people still comply. What worries me, and I used to say this when I would go to international meetings, is what happens when I'm driving home at 2 a.m. from the IRS. In most places in the world, if a traffic light's red, at 2 a.m. they'd drive right through it, or they might hesitate a moment. Most Americans would still stop, but I notice some of them running that light. That's just a signal of our behavior patterns, and it worries me.

There's going to be enormous pressure to find revenue in the future.

I used to worry. I would tell the staff, "If, because of our behavior, compliance falls off half of 1%, 1%, that's more than our budget. For God's sake, don't do anything to make it worse. I know how bad it is, I understand that. But if we did something that made it worse by our own action or misbehavior—just don't make it worse." I would bet most of my successors said the same thing or something similar. That's the thing that scares the hell out of me. You're collecting $1.7 trillion, $1.8 trillion—no, it's almost $2 trillion now. One percent of that is a huge amount of money.

Endnotes

1.   "The 10 deadly sins" refers to provisions of the Revenue Reform Act of 1998 that set severe penalties for IRS employees who violated certain regulations in their dealings with taxpayers. The possibility that spurious charges made by taxpayers could lead to wrongful application of such penalties is said by some to hamper appropriate tax enforcement practices at the IRS.

2.   Expensing of stock options refers to a business firm's accounting treatment of the provision of stock options as part of employee compensation. A stock option is a contract that allows the recipient to buy or sell stock at a predetermined price at some future date. Such options are an implicit cost to the issuing firm, but in the past, firms have not always recognized such costs in their accounting. If such a cost is recorded as a cost at the time the option is issued, it is said to be "expensed." Alternatively, it might not be recorded until the employee exercises the option, in other words, when he uses the contract to buy or sell the company's stock. A firm that employs the use of stock options and expenses such options will record lower profits than if it delayed recognizing the options until they were exercised by the employee.

3.   "Carryover basis" refers to rules on the tax that applies to capital gains. The "basis" of a financial asset is its cost to the purchaser. The capital gain is the difference between the sale price of the asset and its basis. If an asset is not sold by the purchaser, but transferred as a gift or as part of an estate, there is currently no income tax due from the original owner or from the recipient. For the recipient of the asset, the asset is assigned a basis equal to its market value at the time of transfer, and capital gains taxes are due on appreciation above the level of the new basis. Under current legislation for repeal of the Estate Tax, the basis of an asset in this situation would be redefined for tax purposes as the original purchase price, hence the term "carryover basis." This means a higher tax burden on the recipient of the asset in the event the asset has appreciated at all since its original purchase.

4.   Joel Slemrod and Bill Gale. "We Tax Dead People." Washington, D.C.: The Brookings Institution.

5.   "Pay-go" refers to budget rules that require spending increases in one area to be offset by spending cuts elsewhere.

6.   Cohen is referring to the Earned Income Tax Credit, a refundable credit primarily for low-income working families with children.

7.   Michael Graetz. 2005. "A Fair and Balanced Tax System for the 21st Century," *Toward Fundamental Tax Reform*, Alan J. Auerbach and Kevin A. Hassett (eds). Washington, D.C.: AEI Press, American Enterprise Institute.

8.   Robert Greenstein and Iris Lav, "The Graetz Tax Reform Plan and the Treatment of Low-Income Households," Center on Budget and Policy Priorities, June 27, 2005.

9.   "P-A-Y-E" stands for pay as you earn, and it refers to the system of income taxation in the United Kingdom, one which minimizes compliance burdens on taxpayers.

CHAPTER 3

Interview: Donald C. Alexander

Max B. Sawicky interviews Donald C. Alexander, former commissioner of the Internal Revenue Service under President Richard Nixon.

Joining the IRS

When did you begin working for the IRS?

In March 1973, after I was nominated, but before I was confirmed.

That was the Nixon administration.

That's right. President Nixon appointed me.

Had you been in private practice before then?

I'd been in private practice, and I had been very active in the American Bar Association tax section. I had made a lot of speeches and written a lot of articles. When Randolph Thrower was appointed by Nixon, when Nixon was first elected, Randolph asked me to be chief counsel of the service. However, Bob Taft, then a senator from Ohio, was not happy with me and put a hold on my nomination. So it was withdrawn. Otherwise I would have been chief counsel of the IRS in 1969.

What was Taft's misgiving?

I had moved from his law firm to a competing firm and a lot of business moved with me.

So it wasn't exactly high principle?

I don't think that it was high principle. I think it was some other reason.

Basic concerns in tax compliance

What problems do we have with tax compliance now? Broadly speaking, what's the most important priority for addressing it?

We have a systemic failure on the part of a large number of taxpayers to comply with their obligations to the system. We have addressed that in part under Commissioner Mark Everson's tenure. It needs more attention, much more. It needs more work by the IRS, it needs more resources in the IRS, and it needs to have some assistance from Congress by not loading even more tax expenditures into the Internal Revenue Code.

Is compliance worse now than ever? Is there some trend that you see as a growing problem, or has it always been as bad as it is now, more or less?

I think that it was worse a few years ago when IRS Commissioner Charles Rossotti shamefully neglected compliance. He was pushed into his position by the Congress, the Senate Finance Committee in particular. I think compliance is better now. In the corporate community it certainly is better than it was a few years ago. A few years ago I'd say it was as low as it's ever been, and much lower than it was in the past two decades.

The Revenue Reform Act of 1998 (RRA)

We had the Revenue Reform Act in 1998. How would you assess its impact on the IRS's success in fulfilling its mandate?

I think that it had an enormous adverse impact on the IRS. The IRS was basically directed by Congress not to do its job. The IRS was directed to assist taxpayers to fulfill their responsibilities, but to lay off making taxpayers fulfill their responsibilities if they didn't want to do it. The IRS was told that "Compliance 2000," a notion espoused by a former commissioner, was the way to go. That notion was that an educated taxpayer will comply. A taxpayer happy with the IRS will comply.

Was that Commissioner Rossotti?

No, that was Fred Goldberg. Goldberg sold this to the commission that looked into the IRS and that led to the 1998 act. Commissioner Goldberg, I think, genuinely believed the idea that what he called "strong-armed compliance" didn't work, and that you should help taxpayers and they would comply. I think that he genuinely believed that, for a while anyway. I didn't believe it, nor did Peggy Richardson.[1] But unfortunately, former Senator Robert Kerrey (D-Neb.) and to some extent former Congressman Rob Portman (R-Ohio) believed it. That led to the hearings preceding the 1998 act, hearings that were simply staged with witnesses who, if they didn't commit perjury, at least grossly exaggerated. The 1998 act was a vast overreaction.

There was a Government Accountability Office (GAO) report on the hearings reported in Tax Notes. *I don't know if that was ever actually released to the public.*

I think it wasn't. I think that the people that staged the hearing forbade the release. The people that staged the hearing refused to let the IRS respond to these exaggerations. Senator Roth stated that the IRS had done enough to destroy lives; he wasn't going to permit any more to be done. Of course, that's a wonderful way of saying that somebody can claim that he saw a man leering at his daughter taking a shower, when the guy was actually in Jamaica and the daughter was in Florida.

You could say the refusal to release the report was pretty damning in and of itself.

It certainly was.

There was not any dispute that there was a report, I take it.

It's a tribute to the integrity of the GAO that they could actually put together a report that would make it pretty clear that these stories were grossly exaggerated, if not simply made up.

Specifically, what activities were curbed or discouraged or terminated because of the 1998 act, in favor of what sort of other activities?

There were several things. One is simply the IRS's resources and what the IRS is supposed to do. The thrust of the act was to tell the IRS that it had to do much more in taxpayer service and therefore much less in making taxpayers comply. The specifically disfavored activities were seizures on the collection side. The IRS was told that it shouldn't go around seizing taxpayers' property to pay overdue and unpaid taxes, and it has complied with that. Seizures have gone from several thousands down to a few hundred and are still way down.

The circumstances in which the IRS seizes property have greatly changed. Among other collection activities not as strong as seizures—levies and liens—the IRS has taken far fewer actions then it took in the past. Taxpayers, of course, are fully aware of that and, I think, are taking advantage. Regarding examinations and criminal investigation, the IRS was told that it should de-emphasize those compliance activities.

And the IRS's resources—which are largely people—were directed to serve the taxpayer, and serving the taxpayer did not include, at that time anyway, the idea of auditing a taxpayer. So audits decreased greatly and criminal investigations decreased greatly. Collection actions decreased hugely, because of the IRS's direction with this Compliance 2000 notion that hard-nosed compliance should not be undertaken.

Should the RRA be repealed altogether? Is the main problem the infamous section 1203, the "10 deadly sins?"[2]   What would be the best focus in terms of looking back at that?

It shouldn't be repealed altogether. Some of it actually makes sense. The "10 deadly sins" provision ought to be repealed. I don't know of any satisfactory way to fix it. They tried to fix it a little bit, but it has no business being in the law. One, it's unnecessary, and two, it's inadvisable. Some of the collection due process provisions ought to be reviewed carefully to see if they really make sense, and if they impede collection more than they protect taxpayers. Generally, it ought to be reviewed very carefully to see whether it should be modified, whether some provisions should be removed, and whether it has served a useful purpose.

There's one provision that I find particularly of interest. It requires anyone appointed to be commissioner of Internal Revenue to demonstrate prior managerial experience and abilities. That was put in I think in an effort to make sure that somebody like me could never be commissioner again. The only managerial experience that I had was sort of co-managing a Cincinnati law firm (a fairly big one, but small by Washington or New York standards), and also managing the lives of about 150 people in World War II. Maybe that doesn't count; it probably doesn't. That rule has not served the country very well, unless one agrees that Mr. Rossotti was the best commissioner that we've ever had. While Mr. Everson is a good commissioner on the right track, I don't think that his prior running of Sky Chefs necessarily made him a good commissioner. I think that Larry Gibbs was an excellent commissioner, and I don't think that he had much in the way of outside, demonstrated experience in management. That's a stupid provision designed, I think, to make sure that some of us (I'm perhaps the prime example) knew our place, because I spoke up in 1998 and 1997 and others did not.

Is it biasing appointments towards the private sector? I guess you could be a public sector manager and qualify in that context.

I'm not sure that would count. If public sector management counts, then what's more important than leading people who put their lives on the line every day, as my outfit certainly did in World War II?

What has been the effect of the "10 deadly sins" provision of the Act on the IRS functioning? What evidence is there for its dysfunctional effect on the IRS?

I think GAO could speak to that a lot better than I can. I think they've studied the "10 deadly sins" provision and its effect on morale. Its effect on collection morale was basically to stop enforcement actions. If you don't do anything you can't get into trouble. If you do something, you might. So the idea is to not do anything.

That's where the incentives point?

Right. And when the commissioner has a non-delegable right to relieve someone of the problem that the person would otherwise have in an asserted violation of the ten deadly sins, you have an unworkable structure.

IRS abuse and abuse of IRS

Seizure has been the source of IRS horror stories. Is there any evidence on the extent of improper seizures in the history of the IRS?

Oh yes, a lot. In the IRS, a seizure is sort of the final act. Once you take property forcibly from a taxpayer, that is a very strong action indeed. Everyone at the job that I had up until the 1990s, and I'm including Peggy Richardson in that group, worried about examples (and there were a few) of overzealous agents. There were more overzealous agents in the criminal investigation area where the IRS sometimes would go on raids with other agencies. Raids should be undertaken only when there is very, very careful thought ahead of time as to why IRS is doing this, and as to the repercussions if some of the assumptions that give rise to the raid are wrong.

All of us at headquarters attempted, with some degree of success and some degree of failure, to try to make sure that the IRS's powers, very strong powers indeed, were used very, very carefully. That didn't mean that there weren't errors from time to time; there were.

Do you think that the errors were random, or was there any pattern in terms of responsibility? Is there anybody we could point to as more zealous than warranted as administrator?

In particular localities there were particular people that were over-zealous. For instance, when I was commissioner, the Miami office had a reputation—well-deserved—of being overzealous. I made some personnel changes for that reason. I got into deep trouble.

I was accused of taking actions to help particular former clients. I was accused of being personally involved in trying to save people who warranted no salvation. I went before two grand juries: a grand jury in Washington for an entire afternoon where most of the grand jurors were asleep, and a grand jury in Miami, because I took an interest in trying to curb what I thought was highly improper use of the IRS's resources in Miami.

I may be the only one who ever questioned himself before a grand jury. The Department of Justice people conducting it found that the grand jury, and particularly the foreman of the grand jury, thought I was right and was trying to do my job right. They thought there was absolutely nothing to this hilarious story that a couple of people that couldn't stand each other, whom I had known in Cincinnati, were out on Francis Langford's huge boat with me to fix a $30,000 collection case. It would have taken more than $30,000 to get the boat out of the harbor.

The foreman and I had lunch. The Justice people never even asked me about that allegation all morning. They were thinking of taking me to another grand jury somewhere. The foreman forbade me to question myself in the early afternoon. The Justice objected. The foreman over-ruled the objection, provided they question me thoroughly about that particular allegation. They questioned me about that particular allegation which was totally false, and that was the end of it.

Today you would be a hero for something like that.

Strangely enough, I cared about civil rights, I cared about taxpayers' rights. But I also cared about enforcement of the tax laws.

Was there any partisan political background to this?

Oh yes, there was quite a bit. I made the mistake of asking for oversight because President Nixon became quite unhappy with me. I thought that oversight would be a good idea because I wanted to keep my job for a while, and I wanted to do the job. Bella Abzug and Ben Rosenthal, among others, decided they would help the Government Operations Committee look into the IRS. They did and had some real fun. That was partisan. The Ways and Means Committee's Oversight Subcommittee (run by Congressman Charles Vanik from Ohio) was partisan. The Ways and Means Committee was absolutely not, nor was the Senate Finance Committee.

Social programs in the tax code

On the tax expenditure front, you made the point that these programs would be better administered by other departments. Let's take an example: any sort of refundable credit that involves cash for children. Supposing this was given to the Department of Health and Human Services (HHS). If the credit is income-tested, in effect it's a negative income tax with conditions. In that circumstance, wouldn't they need to interface with the IRS? In a sense they're administering their own income tax and they need the same sort of information. Doesn't that create a different sort of problem, and suggest that there is a case for that administration being consolidated, at least in that example? There are other examples that would raise other issues.

The Child Tax Credit and the Earned Income Credit (EIC) do interplay with the computation of income because a taxpayer's income in the broad sense is one of the measuring factors of entitlement. Food stamps, of course, have somewhat the same situation. Welfare payments have somewhat the same situation. If you're Paris Hilton you're not entitled to welfare payments. Therefore, proving entitlement to welfare needs some sort of registration and some sort of check on that registration.

Is the IRS the appropriate entity to administer it because of that connection? I think not. I fought that and lost on the EIC. I think that the IRS should not have administered the EIC; it should have been administered by HHS. HHS does have the responsibility of administering some of the payments that are made to deserving people who have families and who don't have enough income to support their families. Congress is, I think, right in assisting those people, just as they provide food stamps for those people.

I think that social workers can do a far better job than the IRS can of administering a social program like that. I lost, because I think President Nixon wanted to have an EIC and Milton Friedman wanted to have a negative income tax. I think that more attention was paid to Milton Friedman than to me.

Pressing a little bit on that, assuming the HHS is administering it, don't they have to reach out to the IRS to verify income information?

They don't on food stamps and the like. If they wanted to make sure that Paris Hilton wasn't collecting the EIC, that's one of the ways of making that determination: not a self-certification process, but another process. But these people that we're talking about would not be filing tax returns in the first place; many of them would not be. So the IRS wouldn't have the information unless the IRS was required to keep it for this special purpose.

The IRS at last has a program going on something that I tried to get and couldn't: pre-certification. The IRS was told to lay off. That's terrible. The IRS was told, "Hey, you can't do this, because it's unfair to these people." Right now, of course, it would be impossible to remove the EIC because of those who favor it and the concept behind it: to supplement the income of people who are trying to move from welfare to work. It's a great idea. They're afraid that if you had to appropriate the money, the money wouldn't be appropriated. So our Taxpayer Advocate and I have discussed this and, needless to say, we are on quite opposite sides.

There are some tax expenditures that have virtually nothing to do with taxes and are just run through the income tax.

Oh, a lot of them. The IRS is administering at least half of our discretionary expenditures now. The budget calls for about $1.8 trillion of discretionary expenditures and the IRS is administering half of it: $900 billion at least. It's incredible. Congress asks for that every time, but every Congress adds to the IRS's burden, and then they ask, "Why are the forms so complicated?"

Service versus enforcement

Commissioner Rossotti talked about the idea that taxpayers are customers. Are taxpayers customers?

No, they're not customers. I think that he inherited that from Commissioner Goldberg. A customer can refuse to deal with the other party. A customer can go elsewhere. Taxpayers aren't customers. They ought to be treated faily and with respect and courtesy, but they are not customers. They never have been and never will be.

You said there's been a disproportionate shift in emphasis to service. Clearly, some service is essential and promotes compliance. What kind of service are you meaning? Are we doing too much service now? Or is it simply not enough enforcement? Could we do more service or a different kind of service profitably?

Take an example: the commissioner proposes to close a number of the walk-in offices. I was in favor of those walk-in offices; I wanted them. I didn't like the idea of the IRS saying, "Hey, individual, you must file a return, but by the way we're not going to help you file it." I thought that was an impossible thing and the wrong thing. So I was all for those offices. In fact, some of the tax preparation companies were solidly against that idea because they thought it was taking business away from them, and they made it pretty clear that that shouldn't be done and fought the appropriation.

Things have changed since then. Sure, the IRS needs to assist taxpayers. And it needs to assist taxpayers who can't afford to go to a tax preparer, and even taxpayers who can afford it, but don't want to. Going back to my simple illustration, I didn't think that the IRS could tell taxpayers that they must file and they must file accurately without assisting taxpayers to file and to file accurately.

But how much can you do and how do you do it? You try to do it in the way that you can do the most to help people at the lowest cost. And if walk-in offices are not being used, well then they ought to be combined and there ought to be fewer of them. And now that we have the internet, communication is a lot easier for the people who know how to use it, but it's still difficult for the people who don't.

Tools of tax administration and the small business problem

In some research, taxpayer compliance is directly related to whether you can verify information with third parties, whether there is withholding, and what sort of document matching is possible. Where could this be profitably expanded, and how important would it be? How valuable would it be?

It could be very profitably expanded by broadening withholding and by having something directed toward it. But the IRS's major problem now, and it's been a major problem for some time, is probably the use of third-party documents and third-party reporting, including withholding, to deal with the fact that now we have many more income instances, not between an employer and employee, but instead, between two or more parties that have a relationship that is not subject to current withholding.

Withholding is essential to our broad-based tax system. Document matching is next best, but it doesn't work very well. Part of that is the IRS's fault, and part of it's not. More and more businesses are conducted now, not as C-corporations with employees, but instead as pass-through entities with non-employees.[3]

For withholding, we're talking about dividends and interest?

Dividends and interest are pretty well-handled through information returns. One example of what isn't handled through information returns is payments through informal suppliers. The cash economy goes unreported and untaxed.

Those are a lot of small fry though, right?

They are small fry, many of them.

Is it very labor intensive and not necessarily cost effective to chase them?

Some of them are larger fry, and it would be great to have 5% withheld on payments made to third-party suppliers, informal or not. It doesn't mean that you take it down to the last $100 in cash paid to somebody who comes out and repairs the leak in the roof. That's going to go untaxed. But it means when you're talking $10,000 to $100,000, there ought to be some withholding responsibility, because in information returns, a requirement issue would be largely ignored if it weren't accompanied by withholding. The only way that you can have any degree of compliance with the tax laws that's reasonably satisfactory is to have a paper trail.

If there is an information return, is it simply that the IRS doesn't have the resources to act on information it already has?

I said part of it is IRS's fault. Part of it is that the IRS does not match K-1s, and the IRS should match them.[4] There is a great leakage in partnerships. There is a somewhat lesser leakage, I think, in Subchapter-S corporations.[5] The IRS ought to match effectively K-1 information to make sure that the partner reports what the partner should report from the partnership. The IRS has an equal if not greater responsibility to make sure that the partnership reports accurately. The IRS ignored those responsibilities for many years. When I got there they didn't audit any partnership returns. Why not? Because what if the partnership filed in New York, but all the partners lived in New Jersey? Would you give credit to the New Jersey district or to the Manhattan district?

You could always split it.

I got rid of that. At least that's one thing a commissioner can do: get rid of insular problems like that. But there was and still is a great lack of effective compliance activities in the partnership area.

In the context of chasing income that currently is not part of ordinary reporting or withholding, in a book about tax reform years in 1984, Henry Aaron and Harvey Galper talked about a variation of a cash-flow consumption tax.[6] One of the administrative tools that seems to be relevant to tax administration is a requirement for everyone to have a central account through which all their financial transac-

tions go. That would make it easy for them and for the government to keep track of their income. Do you think that there is any practicality to that?

I don't think that Congress would be willing to require that. I think that it's a political judgment that would be unacceptable.

Politics aside, would it work as an administrative device?

I think that it could be made to work, yeah. I think it could work.

If we're going to tax capital income, then it seems hard to escape the relevance of that proposal.

Yes. Maybe we're not going to tax capital income anymore.

Even if we are just taxing consumption, we would benefit from that kind of institution.
In looking at the data on non-compliance, as you have already brought up, the greater offenders are proprietors and informal suppliers. But there is a fairness issue there. For the universe of proprietors, unincorporated business, and S-corporations, what would be the most productive ways to improve compliance in that area? One of the IRS reforms was to set up separate divisions by taxpayer type.

Yes, SB/SE and LSMB[7] and all those wonderful things. By the way, on that one I think chief counsel's office has recognized that completely ignoring geography doesn't make much sense. So they're going back to an organizational regime that takes geography into account. Sooner or later the IRS will have to do the same thing. But that's an aside.

About addressing compliance among small business proprietors, S-corporations, informal suppliers...

Yes, I mentioned several things. One is extension of withholding at a low rate. That is perhaps politically impossible. It would be a very good idea if it could be done. The other is having effective document matching between the entity, the partnership or Subchapter-S entity, and its owners. The third is to have an effective audit program of partnership entities, entities that are pass-through entities to the same extent as if they were corporate entities, because document matching tells you only what the partnership 1065 return has reported. It doesn't tell you whether that report was correct.

So you have to have an effective audit program. And they don't have one yet. You have to have effective document matching. They are getting there, but they're not there yet.

What about for the smaller fry, the self-employed, mom-and-pop institutions?

That would be the last thing you would want to go to, because even though there is probably a substantial percentage problem there of what should be reported and what is reported, if they reported everything they should have reported, it still doesn't have much revenue effect.

Not to mention raising a gigantic political firestorm.

Huge, huge political problem. The self-employed have a vested interest in tax avoidance, and they think that it's depriving them of some sort of Constitutional right if you actually do something about coping with the tax avoidance problem. Of course, international opportunities for cheating are very large. Instead of having little bitty amounts, like the guy that fixes the leak in the roof for $100 and doesn't pay any tax on the hundred dollars, here we're talking about the guy that has $5 million and shifts it to the Caymans and doesn't pay any tax on the $5 million, which was entirely income.

Privatization and tax administration

I'm struck by the extent of information the IRS already has that it could use. It's one thing to say, "Well, we don't know, and we can't go after what we don't know about." But there is information that they have which evidently is not exploited and has already been testified to by people. There are literal debts that they are aware of that they simply don't collect.

Oh, yes. In the collection area a lot goes uncollected that absolutely should be collected. Part of it is that the IRS gets there too late, part of it is that the IRS has insufficient resources, and part of it is that the IRS maybe doesn't utilize its resources as well as it should. But the solution to the collection problem is not in bringing in private collectors to pick the low-hanging fruit, but instead to give the IRS more resources. The IRS can do far more with those additional resources than any private collector.

Why is that? Why not use private collectors?

There are several reasons, I think. The first is that it is inefficient. If you were to give private collectors $1 billion, you're going to collect far less revenue than if you were to take that $1 billion and provide additional resources for IRS people. Unlike private collectors, the IRS already has the tools and the machinery in place to decide whether something is really low-hanging fruit or whether it's not. The IRS can do a better job without a commission paid to a third party to collect taxes; that's its job.

An economist might translate what you're saying as, "There is a large fixed-cost to getting into this business."

There is a large fixed-cost. The IRS is already in the business. Given as much money as they're going to be taking in this private collection initiative, if the IRS were given more, the IRS could do much more than a private collector would. The private collector people, I think, admit that. Then why don't they want to give the IRS more money? That's the idea that we've got to starve the beast, reduce the size of government by denying it resources, which is a perfectly absurd idea. It's the idea that many in the majority party appear to have right now. I hope they get rid of it.

Is there some efficient way the service could work together with private sector outfits like H&R Block to improve taxpayer education and assistance?

There is, and I think they do work together. I think that they do much more than they did in my day. In my day, Henry Block perceived me as being a competitor who was using government money to deprive H&R Block of much-needed revenue. I think the situation is far better these days and that H&R Block is a good citizen now. I think that H&R Block and its competitors furnish a very useful function.

There was a horrible story in Tax Notes *a couple of months ago. They sent a return to six or eight local service centers: H&R Block, Liberty, and a few others. I don't think that they got even one return back that was done properly.[8]*

I'm not at all surprised. Every April somebody will put together some questions, and some of those are trick questions, and they'll take them to six or eight different offices, and they'll get a different response. Once you look at the questions, the differences are easily discovered and are based on the interpretation of the question rather than a clear error, such as you're not entitled to a child credit for your dog. But people love to write that stuff and people love to read it.

They love to play gotcha. So you think that the articles were not as fair as they might have been?

No, never. If they are fair, they're not good articles.

Recreation for journalists?

Oh yeah, it's fun. When have they last told you that an agency is doing their job right and well? That doesn't sell papers.

In terms of education and competition with the private sector, one of the issues in the past has been provision of software. Should the IRS give people free software to do their taxes?

I thought that the IRS had done some things. I thought that they worked together with Block and did produce some useful software, but I don't know. And there, how far do you go? And who are you competing with? Who fulfills this particular need if you don't fill it? Is there a big enough need on the part of people who are genuinely in need for you to produce software in addition to what you are already producing, which is all sorts of ways of trying to tell people what their rights and responsibilities are?

And when you have the annual model changing the law you've got to tell people, "Hey, you've got something new here that you should take advantage of if you qualify, and to qualify you need to meet requirements one through five." Or, "You got something that you've got to look out for, because even though last year it was okay, this year it's not."

You could argue that if the government says you've got to do taxes, they ought to provide you with the means to do them. They give you forms. They don't make you prepare your own forms.

They supply the forms. Software is simply a current version one can argue of the time-honored paper form.

In Maryland, you can do your state income tax on the Web for nothing.

Yes.

The IRS workforce

Do you think IRS employees are paid enough?

No.

Is it attracting the people that it needs, to do what it has to do, aside from the number of people?

I'm surprised and delighted to see a lot of people—like (former senior IRS officials) Dale Collinson and Tom Terry—are willing to go back and work with the IRS. They serve well, to the benefit of the IRS and the country. But IRS people should be paid more. They're accountable for doing their jobs well and working diligently.

Would that apply completely up and down the ranks? Is it more of an executive problem or more of a line problem?

I think that it's a problem for line and executive staff throughout, though some people sit there and don't do very much and manage to last it out. I think good executives are hard to keep because there is a great demand. Not as much, perhaps, as there used to be by the accounting firms, but there is a great demand for IRS people, and a demand for IRS lawyers particularly. It's hard for them to stay when they can make at least double, usually triple, what they are making working for the IRS.

Have you had any experience with unionized sectors of the IRS? Has their role been constructive or otherwise?

I think that it's more constructive than it was back in my day. I couldn't quite understand why the government unions were necessary when you couldn't bargain over wages and hours. And that meant that you bargained over things like how hard people have to work and how many breaks they could take and things like that. I couldn't quite understand that. But then I was coming from the private sector, where I'd never had much experience with unions. I thought the union was simply a burden that one had to bear for some inexplicable reason. I think now the situation has probably changed some. I think the unions are pretty helpful in many respects. For example, the union has come out very strongly against privatization of collection. One would surely expect that from the union. And I think that that happens to be a good thing. The union never supported the IRS in any capacity as far as I can remember when I was with the IRS.

Tax administration and fundamental tax reform

One of the stated priorities of the president this year is tax reform. There are different 'fundamental reforms' being tossed around. I'd like to tick through some of them to see what your reaction would be to their relevance, if any, for administration and compliance. One of the most popular is a flat tax. How much simpler would it be? Is it administrable? How much would it ease the job of the IRS? How much would it improve compliance?

I think two very different things. Number one, a real flat tax, meaning one rate, with very limited exemptions such as credits and deductions and the like (which seem to accompany the flat tax proposals), would be much easier for the IRS to administer than the very complex tax system that we have now. Why? Because we would have fewer credits and fewer deductions.

What I'm talking about is the classic flat tax: there is the postcard where you simply report wages or labor compensation and pension distributions, or maybe not even the latter. The post card has virtually nothing on it except exemptions and a standard deduction. On the company side it's basically a value-added tax (VAT)[9] without whatever is reported on the postcard of labor compensation.

That would be simple for the IRS to administer, but very difficult for the public to understand and comply with. The public has become accustomed to all these things we have in our tax law. And the public would like to see a lower rate, but many taxpayers would not see a lower rate if you wanted to produce the same amount of revenue.

They wouldn't see all their special preferences.

They wouldn't see all their little goodies. The people who didn't have the goodies would not be particularly happy. But the people who lost the goodies would be terribly unhappy. So while the IRS's administrative job would be superficially much simpler, the IRS would be the agency that would be blasted. Remember, the Congress just loves to call the code "the IRS code," pretending that they had nothing to do with it. If they were successful, you could expect the worthies pushing this national sales tax, for instance, to blame the IRS for what they did.

On the company side, assuming you had a VAT with labor compensation pulled out, it's been suggested that the ease of doing VAT administration has been overstated.

There's some non-compliance with the credit invoice VAT in the European Union (EU), but there is even greater non-compliance with any kind of complex income tax in the EU. So a credit invoice value-added tax or the like would be much easier for the IRS to administer than the present complex income tax that we have. I think there is much to be said for a credit invoice VAT. A lot of members of Congress—if they talk about a VAT at all—talk about a subtraction VAT because they know that it's more difficult to administer, and they don't want to have something easier to administer. This is the 'starve the beast' group again.

What are the main problems in subtraction VAT administration?

You don't have the line of payers. What that means is that instead of having each party to the overall transaction from the beginning to the end bearing part of the burden, you've got the entire burden placed on one party, with the other parties being subtracted out. That doesn't make for the extreme difficulties of a national retail sales tax (which can't be administered), but it does make it more difficult to administer.

One of the issues with this subtraction VAT is if you provide some concession to income from exports. Some have suggested that that makes a subtraction VAT practically a non-starter.

It probably is. If we were going to have a VAT, with the World Trade Organization (WTO) and other problems, we ought to have a VAT that mimics those that are used everywhere else, and that's a credit invoice VAT. I think a subtraction VAT is a non-starter for various reasons.

The national retail sales tax is backed by a popular movement, and there looks to be a lot of money invested in promoting this idea. You've got many fewer taxpayers to watch over. The advocates have said there wouldn't be an IRS, but let's put that aside for a second. Suppose the IRS ran the sales tax, what kind of world would that be?

It would be a world of non-compliance. A national retail sales tax, replacing the taxes that it's supposed to replace, HR25, is completely un-administrable by the IRS or anybody else. It's clearly un-administrable if the IRS is abolished because the states couldn't possibly administer it.

Why couldn't the IRS do it?

The IRS couldn't do it because there is no way the IRS could force people to pay what they should pay in a national retail sales tax at, say, a 50% tax-exclusive rate or a 30% tax-inclusive rate.[10] The tax is so huge in comparison with a transaction that it puts an impossible burden on the two parties to be honest in their relationships with the party that isn't there, the government, which wants a third, a fourth, a fifth, or half of the sale price. So street merchants right now don't pay sales taxes. So what? The street merchant problem would be magnified a thousand fold if we were to have a national retail sales tax. That's the reason that no country has been able to enact one and administer one.

Would it be any worse with the states or just equally untenable?

It would be a lot worse in the states. The states have big enough problems now. With the value of evasion going up tenfold, people aren't going to pay it, and the IRS can't enforce it. Some years ago, back in the WWII days, we had a whole series of federal excise taxes. Most of them were imposed on manufacturers and the like, where it was possible to collect them. Even then there was a great compliance problem.

There is the Sam Nunn-Pete Domenici model, sometimes called a cash-flow tax or direct consumption tax, wherein you would report all sales or financial assets as income, and they would be in the tax base. Purchases of assets would be deductions. Otherwise, you would be reporting more or less what you report now in terms of income, with fewer credits and other kinds of separate programs that we've already discussed. Politics aside, how does the feasibility of that look to you as a replacement for the income tax?

Theoretically, it stands up reasonably well. However, I can't get past the politics. I don't think that anything like that could ever be enacted.

What would be the main political objections?

What it was before, when Nunn and Domenici brought it out. It did not have many co-sponsors. I think that people saw little benefit in this kind of tax compared to its competitor, the credit invoice VAT.

Why are you going to have this thing? People saw a huge cost in permitting immediate expensing, other than maybe Ernie Christian.[11] Gosh, I figured if Ernie is for it, I better be against it.

Would you care to elaborate on that?

Ernie's a fine guy. But he genuinely believes that somehow you should not tax income from capital. This is a way of keeping it from being taxed. I believe that income from capital should be taxed just as income from services is taxed. The notion that we have a double tax—Grover Norquist said it's taxed four or five times already when he was trying to get rid of the estate tax—is simply false. The largest element of property and wealth in this country, far from being subjected to two or more taxes, is not even subjected to one tax, because it's unrealized appreciation.

On the surface, the Nunn-Domenici model would seem to have some greater practicality. In principle, you could have some kind of concession for housing. It's hard to imagine a reform that leaves housing behind. You could accommodate interest groups to an extent without the thing completely falling apart, and you have this implicit shift to a regime of no taxation of savings or of capital. On the surface it seems like that might have a bigger chance than a flat tax, which is a more radical change, or a sales tax. So why wouldn't the business community be a lot more interested in a Nunn-Domenici–type approach than they seem to have been so far?

Maybe some of them didn't understand it. Maybe some of them didn't take it very seriously. Maybe some of them thought that by the time you excepted out the all elements that you mentioned, that you would have to have such a high rate on the rest of it that you would be in a worse situation than the situation that we're in already. It was about the same time that we were going through this 10-5-3 revolution. That great economist Jack Kemp[12] was proposing to leave our current tax system basically the way it is, but expense everything. They would go that far. I think that the business community saw that as a wonderful way of zeroing out taxes, at the corporate level at least, and that is exactly what happened in the 1981 act.

There was an easier, quicker way for them to get what they wanted.

There was an easier way: we don't have to go into this brave new world that we don't trust anyway to make some changes. At that point there was a genuine interest in writing off plant and equipment, and particularly real estate, and the question was how quickly you write them off. If you put a 10-year life on something that has an economic life of 50 years, you've not only zeroed out your tax on that particular part of your business, but you've also pretty well zeroed your tax on all the other parts.

You're giving away money.

Absolutely. That's exactly what they were doing in 1981; that's the reason for recovering revenue in the 1982 act and the 1984 act. In 1981 we were going broke.

Rather than embrace a clean model that would zero out capital taxes, they went for a quick fix.

That's right. Now, of course, we have a different world because people aren't buying things like plant and equipment anymore. Instead they're using their capital to keep the price of their stock up. Look at what they're doing with excess funds.

The Federal Estate and Gift Tax

How much have you had to do with the Estate and Gift Tax?

Some. I used to practice across the field in Cincinnati, and at that time I had a lot of experience. Lately, I have gotten out of that area for various reasons, one of them being that you could do only so much in this world and another being that I did not like the idea of these family partnerships. I thought it was crooked, and I wasn't going to participate in it.

Is it your impression that the bigger problem with the estate tax is avoidance opportunities or outright evasion?

Avoidance opportunities.

Because there are so many holes in it.

There are so many holes and to some extent the courts have abdicated their responsibility to close those holes. They take these family partnerships seriously, even though the partnership consists of the senior partner or dominant person's wealth represented by publicly traded securities, and treat it as a genuine partnership, but feel it's not.

Could you explain a little bit more how that works, what the gimmick is?

The promoters in this field are largely tax practitioners, mostly lawyers, but the accounting firms are not far behind. (The accounting firms are ahead of lawyers in the regular tax shelters, way ahead.) They tell you that you can remove all taxes from your $10 million estate if you create their family partnership. But you can still control the partnership. The way to do it is to simply transfer what you own into this partnership with your spouse (if you trust him or her), children and the like that are the partners, and suddenly you claim a 30% or 40% or 60% discount. Why? Because all you have is a partnership interest. And all they have is a partnership interest. And by creating this partnership and transferring these rights, you've suddenly reduced your $10 million to say $4 million. And I didn't think that was legal.

And presumably these have eternal life so there is no estate tax?

If you are in the right state, say Delaware, where you could have a dynasty trust, the combination of the dynasty trust and the family partnership means that not only do you have no tax now, but you have no tax forever. Of course, you keep control from the grave for the next 60 years, and all your children turn out to be exactly the way you expected. They all live happily on all that money you've saved from foregone taxes.

The average person hearing that might say that's why we need a flat tax. How does a flat tax address or not address that?

It doesn't address this situation at all, because this is disposing of property and not income. Luckily, the courts at last have turned around a bit, I'm glad to say. They say that these partnerships are facades, they are not real partnerships, and therefore you do not have this 60% discount. They say, "Give them a discount, but a small one." But this is a long explanation of one of the reasons why I got out of that business completely.

If we repeal the estate tax, then that business disappears?

Yeah, that's about the only good reason for repeal.

Maybe the practitioners in that business would object to their repeal of the estate tax.

Oh, they certainly do. But I think that the repeal of the estate tax is a very bad idea.

Conclusion: Policy priorities in tax administration

What would be your top four or five priorities for improving compliance?

First would be to simplify the Internal Revenue Code. Next would be to move tax expenditures to the departments that have the authority and the duty to fulfill the particular responsibility that's in the tax expenditure; HHS would be a great one. There are a lot of others, like the Department of Education. I would like to see more Pell grants and fewer tax credits. The Pell grants can be measured; each year you find out how much they cost, and what they did. Tax expenditures, once enacted, are forgotten and nobody looks at them, with rare exceptions.

That's partly the appeal of them. It's not a bug; it's a feature.

It appeals to those who are pushing them. I'd like to simplify the internal revenue code first, above all things. And I'd like to have a progressive income tax that taxed income from capital as well as income from services. Before, as you know, we had a 70% rate on capital income and a 50% rate on income from services. We valued income from services higher than we did income from capital. Now we've made this enormous change, and we justify it by a mantra that consists of "this is going to make for economic growth," without any proof whatsoever that it indeed does make for economic growth.

One of the economist's standard concerns is that income is intrinsically harder to measure than cash flow in the case of assets and depreciation.

It probably is, because you've got to take certain costs and measure them by a period of one year. You need that one-year period because income tax won't work without some sort of measuring period. The measuring period needn't be one year; it could be six months or two years. My guess is that cash flow is the only reason why one year is useful: you need to have a period where something comes into the federal treasury.

The next thing would be give the IRS adequate resources to do its job. And finally, hold the IRS accountable for doing its job.

On accountability, there is at least what looks like a campaign in the administration to organize systems to rate performance. Are there things that could be measured in the IRS and used in a more precise way than is currently done to rate and reward performance, or to penalize as the case may be?

Unfortunately, the things that you can measure are quite significant to the tax system, but they do lend themselves to the argument made by Fred Goldberg: you get what you measure. Therefore, if you measure what Commissioner Everson is saying, that we have an additional $50 million thanks to our compliance efforts, Goldberg is going to scream that what that means is excessive, heavy-handed enforcement, ignoring taxpayers' rights. And he's got a point to some extent, only to a very limited extent. So you have to do two things: number one is to insist on performance, but number two is to insist on the preservation and respect for our taxpayers' rights. The two are difficult to reconcile.

What measurements would lend themselves to that?

Unfortunately, very few. What you need to have there is a watcher. Right now, who are our watchers? The Government Accountability Office (GAO) has always been a watcher and, I think, a very capable watcher. We do have another one in the Treasury Inspector General for Tax Administration (TIGTA) in the Treasury. I think that it has too many people, and I'm not sure that it's very effective. But you need to have somebody there with the duty to look at the IRS, to make sure that it's not overzealous.

Don't forget the Taxpayer Advocate.

Right. I should have noted the Taxpayer Advocate when I was listing the watchers. The Taxpayer Advocate is the third one. I think the Taxpayer Advocate is a very useful office, and some good came out of the 1998 act. I think that Nina Olsen speaking up is a good thing for the tax system. TIGTA has too many people. The GAO is really not enough. The GAO does a very good, constructive, and fair job in its work of looking at the IRS and looking at the other agencies, and it has in the past as well.

If, as you suggest, a lot of programs were moved into other departments, how much more possible or conceivable would it make the idea of a return-free system or a self-completing system?

We could have a return-free system, but we can't have it under the present conditions. If we were to move the ornaments out of the system and put them where they properly belong, the system could be return-free, not for everybody, but for perhaps the majority of individual taxpayers. The returns themselves would go back to the simpler returns that we had back in the 1960s, when you really did have a very simple return. The whole 1040 wasn't as large as the 1040A or 1040EZ is today. I would have never used the EZ.

Endnotes

1.   Margaret Milner ("Peggy") Richardson was commissioner of the IRS from 1993 to 1997.

2.   The "10 deadly sins" refers to actions under the RRA that can cause IRS employees to be subject to severe penalties. Supporters of the law claim the language safeguards taxpayer rights, while critics charge that it impedes vigorous enforcement of tax law.

3.   "C-corp" refers to Subchapter C of the Internal Revenue Code, according to which a business firm organized as a "C-corp" corporation, or standard business corporation, must pay federal corporate income tax. By contrast, under "S-corp" status, such a requirement does not apply. S-corps are one type of "pass-through" entity. Partnerships are another type. The name refers to the firm's function of passing its net income and associated income tax liability through to those with an ownership interest in the firm. The firm or entity does not pay the tax.

4.   Schedule K-1 is a form filed to report an individual's share of income from participation in a business partnership.

5.   Subchapter-S is a form of legal organization for corporations that allows their owners to forego paying the federal corporate income tax.

6.   Aaron, Henry J. and Harvey Galper. 1985. *Assessing Tax Reform*. Washington, D.C.: The Brookings Institution.

7.   SB/SE and LMSB are, respectively, the Small Business/Self-Employed and the Large and Mid-Sized Business branches of the IRS.

8.   Rojas, Warren. 2005. "Six Chain Tax Shops Take Same Tax Data, Build Six Different Returns." *Tax Notes*. Vol. 107. April 18.

9.   A value-added tax is a form of consumption tax. Unlike a sales tax that is paid entirely at the retail level, the VAT is paid at each state of production on the firm's profits and labor compensation, minus its capital expenditures. The impact is thought to be the same as a sales tax. The credit invoice VAT is administered by checking the firms' invoices for sales to and purchases from other firms, which facilitates enforcement. By contrast, a "subtraction VAT" is more similar to a business income tax, in the sense that the government relies on each firm to report the information relevant to its tax liability.

10.   "Tax-inclusive rate" is the rate of a sales tax defined as the ratio of the amount of tax to the price of the taxed product, gross of the tax. Hence, where the one-dollar retail price of a product is taxed at, for instance, 30%, making the gross-of-tax price $1.30, the tax-inclusive rate is 30/130, or 23%, and the "tax-exclusive rate" is 30%.

11.   Ernest Christian is a tax attorney in Washington, D.C. and a long-time advocate of consumption taxation.

12.   "10-5-3" refers to proposals for streamlined depreciation rules under tax cut proposals of the early 1980s made by Rep. Jack Kemp (R-N.Y.) and Senator William Roth (R-Del.).

CHAPTER 4

Tax cheats and their enablers

by Robert S. McIntyre

You . . . can be a millionaire . . . and never pay taxes! You can be a millionaire . . . and never pay taxes!

You say . . . "Steve . . . how can I be a millionaire . . . and never pay taxes?"

First . . . get a million dollars.

Now . . . you say, "Steve . . . what do I say to the tax man when he comes to my door and says, 'You . . . have never paid taxes'?"

Two simple words. Two simple words in the English language: "I forgot!"
—*Steve Martin*, Saturday Night Live, *Jan. 21, 1978*

Introduction

Lots of unscrupulous big corporations and wealthy people are working hard to hide their profits and income from the tax collector. Their schemes are more complicated than Steve Martin's comic infomercial envisioned, but they're just as damaging to our country, and just as reprehensible. In fact, almost three decades after he delivered it, Martin's tax advice needs only minor updating. Add a few zeros to $1,000,000 and change the punch line to "Seven simple words . . . 'I have a note from my lawyer.'"

The culprits are many. The greedy tax dodgers, of course. Their unscrupulous tax advisers, including America's most prestigious accounting firms, biggest banks, and many law firms—who make billions of dollars facilitating evasion and avoidance. But most of all, the blame lies with demagogic lawmakers in Washington, who have turned a blind eye to tax evasion, and have refused to give the Internal Revenue Service—the tax police—the resources to stop the abuses.

Tax dodging takes many forms. There are, of course, legal loopholes enacted by Congress in response to lobbying pressure. Generally termed "incentives," they purport to encourage people or companies to do something socially or economically useful. Then there are potentially legal (but often not) tax shelters—what might be called "roll your own" loopholes to cut taxes in ways that Congress never officially intended. And finally, there's outright cheating—simply failing to report your income or making up deductions.

Distinguishing one from the other isn't always easy. Taking a deduction for donating your old car to charity is perfectly legal, for instance. But making up an inflated value for the deduction is cheating. Moving your money offshore and failing to declare the income it earns is clearly cheating if you're a person. But it may be a legal—or at least quasi-legal—tax shelter if you're a multinational corporation.

Likewise, how do you tell a tax shelter from an authorized tax incentive? One rule of thumb might be that "incentives" are tax breaks lobbied into the law fair and square by corporations and people seeking public subsidies for doing what they'd do anyway. (Would-be tax avoiders don't lobby Congress to pay them to change their conduct—that would be silly.) In contrast, shelters are abuses of the tax laws that nobody paid Congress to allow. Is one more despicable than the other? I suppose you could say that if something is so ridiculous that even the most corrupt Congress can't countenance it, then maybe it's worse. Or maybe not. Bill Thomas, the California Republican who chairs the House Ways and Means Committee these days, doesn't seem to be able to tell the difference, and I've always found him to be pretty clearheaded, albeit poorly intentioned.

In the realm of tax shelters, tax lawyers like to draw a sharp distinction between tax avoidance and tax evasion. The former is what they do for a living, whereas the latter is shameful criminal behavior. More precisely, the lawyers call a scheme "avoidance" if it has a reasonable chance of being upheld if the IRS ever detects it. In contrast, they say, "evasion" depends on the IRS never finding out what's going on.

But given how few tax returns our cash-strapped IRS now audits, the reward-to-risk ratio for playing the audit lottery with extremely shady tax shelter schemes is very high. In fact, an illustration of Gresham's Law seems to have occurred in the tax field. Just as bad money drives out good in an unregulated market, bad tax advisors can drive out good ones. Accounting firms that don't market tax shelters fear they'll lose customers to their competitors. Tax lawyers who honorably refuse to write letters blessing dubious shelters—an essential insurance policy for tax avoiders against being criminally charged if a scheme is detected and rejected by the IRS—find their clients shifting to less principled attorneys.

In fact, all of the major accounting firms, including Ernst & Young, Deloitte Touche, PricewaterhouseCoopers, and KPMG, have been involved in marketing clearly abusive tax shelters. So have many supposedly respectable law firms. Numerous large banks and investment firms, such as Citigroup, Bank of America, Wachovia, and Merrill Lynch, have also been implicated in tax evasion and/or aggressive sheltering activities.

The more dubious the scheme, the more the lawyers and accountants charge their clients: "My own recommendation is that we should be paid a lot of money here for our opinion since the transaction is clearly one that the IRS would view as falling squarely within the tax shelter orbit," a KPMG tax advisor told the firm in May of 1999 (as a Senate investigation revealed this February).

Far too many investors and business owners are tempted to understate their gross business receipts and/or overstate their expenses, move their investments offshore, fail to report their capital gains accurately, and so forth. Not all succumb, of course. Even for those who do, the actual alchemy of making income disappear for tax purposes is probably often a mystery. That doesn't in any way absolve the tax cheats and aggressive avoiders from blame: they're the demand side of the equation. But without the supply side, the lawyers, accountants, and banks that set up the shelters, the demand would go unrequited.

The ethically challenged tax advisers who are willing to help would-be tax evaders are well aware that the chances of their clients being audited by the IRS are extremely low, so long as a tax return doesn't raise obvious red flags. Their chief weapons to win this "audit lottery" are complexity and subterfuge.

In contrast, the vast majority of Americans who make almost all their money from wages have few opportunities for serious tax cheating. Taxes are withheld from paychecks, W-2 forms are easily matched against tax returns, and straightforward deductions for mortgage interest, state and local taxes, and (most) charitable donations are easily checked for accuracy.

So the majority of us who honestly pay our taxes have a major stake in getting the tax dodgers to ante up, too—hundreds of billions of dollars a year, in fact, although no one knows the exact amount for sure.

Taxes, as Supreme Court Justice Oliver Wendell Holmes noted a century ago, are "the price of civilization." Most of us are willing to pay our fair share of the cost of all the things we want and need our government to do—so long as we believe others are chipping in, too. But others—too often those who have gained the most from our society— prefer to shirk their responsibilities and pass the cost onto the rest of us. So let's take a closer look at tax sheltering, starting with individuals and moving on to corporations. And finally, let's then talk about what we can do about it.

> "Anyone may arrange his affairs so that his taxes shall be as low as possible; he is not bound to choose that pattern which best pays the Treasury. There is not even a patriotic duty to increase one's taxes. Over and over again the Courts have said that there is nothing sinister in so arranging affairs as to keep taxes as low as possible. Everyone does it, rich and poor alike and all do right, for nobody owes any public duty to pay more than the law demands."
> —*Judge Learned Hand, writing for the 2nd Circuit Court of Appeals in* Helvering v. Gregory, *69 F.2d 809 (1934)*

Tax shelters for wealthy people

From a distance, the tax code can look like a fine work of art. Its overarching principles, to tax "income from whatever source derived" and to do so at graduated rates, are admirable and sound. But closer up one finds that vandals have been at work. Legislators carve large holes in the system. Lawyers and accountants chip away at small defects until they become big ones. Eventually, new laws are passed and regulations are issued to try to deal with these problems, and so the process continues. The length and complexity of the income tax code is often criticized, but much of that complexity is actually devoted to trying to stop the avoidance and evasion that the vandals have created.

Taken out of context (as it often is on right-wing Web sites), Learned Hand's statement in *Helvering v. Gregory* appears to offer tax sheltering an official stamp of approval. But the actual decision in the *Gregory* case was quite the opposite: it established the principle that activities engaged in solely for tax avoidance should *not* stand up. As the Supreme Court said in affirming the Court of Appeals ruling in favor of the IRS, "the legal right of a taxpayer to decrease the amount of what otherwise would be his taxes, or altogether avoid them, by means which the law permits, cannot be doubted. . . . But the question for determination is whether what was done, apart from the tax motive, was the thing which the statute intended."

In a later decision in 1949, Hand himself made the principle even clearer: "The doctrine of *Gregory v. Helvering* . . . means that in construing words of a tax statute which describes commercial or industrial transactions we are to understand them to refer to transactions entered upon for commercial or industrial purposes and not to include transactions entered upon for no other motive but to escape taxation."

Nevertheless, "transactions entered upon for no other motive but to escape taxation" have continued to be concocted over the years, with their success rate depending on who's been in charge in Washington, D.C. Recently, the tax-shelter problem seems to have reached a new peak.

For historical perspective, let's go back to the 1950s, when the top personal tax rate was a staggering 91%. Only a handful of very wealthy people faced this rate, of course, but for them, the impetus for tax sheltering was enormous, since a dollar saved in taxes was the equivalent of earning $11 before taxes.

Tax shelters got a big boost from the Supreme Court in a 1947 case called *Crane v. Commissioner*, which said that corporations and investors could write off investments financed with borrowed money even if they have no intention of ever repaying it and are not legally obligated to repay it. (Ironically, this disastrous case was a Pyrrhic "victory" for the IRS.) Lawmakers helped the tax shelter industry along by enacting loopholes that could be exploited as shelters. In 1954, for example, "accelerated depreciation" let companies and investors write off business machinery, equipment, real estate, and so forth much faster than they actually wear out. Investors in oil shelters got *immediate* write-offs for their drilling costs, plus "percentage depletion" deductions. The combination of large write-offs and interest deductions was a bonanza for those seeking shelter from taxation.

At first glance, writing off machinery and equipment faster than it actually wears out may not seem like much of a tax break. After all, eventually investors will get to take the full write-offs; accelerated depreciation just speeds them up. Esteemed tax lawyer Sheldon Cohen, who later went on to serve as IRS Commissioner in the Johnson Administration, recalls that when he tried to interest the big accounting firms in depreciation-based tax shelters back in the 1950s, the accountants at first brushed him off. What's the point, they asked. It's merely a tax "deferral."

But as Cohen explained, deferring taxes is a very big deal, indeed. For one thing, there's the time value of money. If the government lets you put off paying your taxes for a year, and you invest the money from the taxes you didn't pay, then after a year you'll at least have the interest of your loan. But the magic of deferring taxes, Cohen pointed out, is much more substantial than that. If you have a foolproof, low-cost scheme to put off paying taxes for a year, then when the year is up, you'll just do it again but in a bigger way. And then again and again and again. Which means you'll never pay taxes as long as the loophole remains open. It all comes down, Sheldon said, to "Cohen's Law": a dollar in taxes deferred is a dollar that the government never collects. Either the original investor will keep finding new deferral schemes, or someone else will take his place.

Once the accounting firms caught on, tax shelters involving equipment leasing flourished. Wealthy people became the nominal owners of boxcars, airplanes, and a variety of other items about which they know little or nothing, and leased them to corporations. In effect, railroads, airlines, and other companies with more tax breaks than they could use sold them to wealthy people, for whom they were very valuable. As an added bonus, when investors sold their boxcars and planes after the depreciation write-offs had played out, they got an additional, huge tax break. Any tax due on the sale was treated as a capital gain, taxed at only 25%. So they saved 91 cents in taxes for every dollar they wrote off, but paid back at only 25 cents on the dollar later. What a deal for them, and what a bad deal for the general public.

Since the 1950s, individual tax sheltering has waxed and waned with the political winds. Reforms in the 1960s and 1970s took much of the oomph out of some kinds of shelters. Ronald Reagan lurched from vastly expanding shelter opportunities in 1981 to closing down most of the worst ones in 1986. (Reagan's budget director, David Stockman, actually promised that Reagan's loophole-ridden 1981 tax-cut bill, by lowering the top marginal tax rate from 70 % to 50%, would "effectively eliminate" the tax shelter industry, despite all the new loopholes—apparently under the theory that no one would mind paying a mere 50% rate. As all rational people predicted, precisely the opposite occurred. But the far right continues to make similar ridiculous claims to this day.)

Starting around the early 1990s, the tax shelter industry staged a remarkable comeback, as promoters moved on to esoteric schemes previously unheard of or only dabbled in. "Those kinds of things, that is not what was happening 10 or 20 years ago," IRS Commissioner Mark Everson told the Senate Finance Committee in June of 2004. "But because we have tightened up on some of the other shelters, now people are finding these channels, and that is very disturbing to us." Many of these schemes rely heavily on keeping the IRS from discovering what's really going on—i.e., they're illegal. So in the 1990s, the tax shelter industry waged a lobbying war against the IRS in Congress. They found a receptive audience, especially among Republicans, and succeeded in both cutting the IRS budget sharply and putting new restraints on enforcement.

How do current shelters work? There are many varieties. But one widespread type of scheme is to undermine a basic principle of the tax law that deductions by one taxpayer should usually generate income for another. If a company pays wages to its employees, it takes a tax deduction while the workers pay taxes. If a business buys products from another business, one has a tax deduction, the other has taxable income. If this principle holds, then the tax law is self-policing to some degree and is certainly less susceptible to systematic abuses.

But what if X gets a deduction for a payment to Y, and Y, for whatever reason, isn't taxable? Then the self-policing system doesn't work. Finding, creating, or concocting a non-taxable Y is the lynchpin of many tax shelters today.

One well-known way to find a non-taxable Y involves offshore tax havens—countries that impose little or no income tax and have strict financial secrecy laws. If a would-be non-taxpayer in the United States can get a deduction for payments to a tax-haven entity he controls, or move income-producing assets offshore, then it becomes very difficult for the IRS to detect his tax evasion. In one recent case where the IRS did break through the veil of secrecy, it uncovered a major offshore tax-shelter scheme facilitated by major banks and credit card companies. The banks helped their clients move money to a offshore tax haven such as the Cayman Islands. Then the credit card companies let the tax avoiders borrow against those assets on their VISA, MasterCard, or American Express card. So rather than paying taxes on their investment income, the customers got to spend it tax-free—at least until they got caught.

Unfortunately, getting caught in offshore tax evasion is the exception rather than the rule. The Tax Justice Network estimates that there are now $11.5 trillion in offshore assets held by wealthy individuals worldwide. This translates into $860 billion a year in untaxed investment income every year, with a $255 billion a year cost to governments around the world. There's no doubt that Americans hold a significant share of these assets.

To be sure, hiding money offshore is usually illegal, at least for people. To keep their offshore assets and income hidden, tax evaders and their facilitators have actually organized a tax cheaters lobby in the United States. It's devoted to keeping up the wall of secrecy that makes it difficult for the IRS and the tax agencies of other governments to discover offshore tax evasion.

This so-called "Center for Freedom and Prosperity" is or has been endorsed by a long list of right-wing luminaries, including former Rep. Jack Kemp (R-N.Y.), former House Majority Leader Dick Armey (R-Tex.), Paul Weyrich of the christian right, Steve Moore, formerly of the Cato Institute, the anti-union National Taxpayers Union, the Heritage Foundation, corporatist groups such as Citizens for a Sound Economy, former Chamber of Commerce chief economist Richard Rahn, supply-side economist Arthur Laffer, and the ubiquitous corporate lobbyist/Republican operative Grover Norquist. One paper on the group's pro-tax-evasion Web site explains, "Why the War on Money Laundering is Counter-productive." Another offers, "The Case for Swiss Bank Secrecy." And still another worries about "the future of offshore financial centres, such as Vanuatu"—a south Pacific tax haven also known for its promotion of pay-per-view pornography scams on the Internet. A recent press release claims that "low tax jurisdictions serve as an escape hatch for over burdened taxpayers"—as if those who evade, rather than pay, their taxes are the overburdened parties.

Lest you think a group that bills itself as a lobby for tax cheats might be an ineffectual bunch of kooks, note that in 2001, it helped persuade the Bush Administration to back out of an agreement among developed countries to pressure tax-haven countries to stop facilitating money laundering, drug dealing and tax evasion. The Clinton Administration had championed this disclosure effort, but soon after George W. Bush took office, his Treasury Department announced that things had changed, and that stopping tax evasion "is not in line with this administration's tax and economic priorities."

Since 9/11, the Bush Administration has become less strident in its support for bank secrecy and other non-disclosure policies. But it continues to oppose the most effective proposals for disclosure.

Cheating on taxes by moving money offshore illegally is not the only way to find a non-taxable Y. For those who prefer to stay closer to home, a non-taxable place to park income sometimes can be found right here in the USA. Take, for example, an array of tax shelters involving tax-exempt entities such as charities. In its simplest form, a charitable shelter would work like this: First, donate a bunch of money to a charity you control. That's deductible (with some limits as to timing). Now borrow the money back and spend it as you wish. Borrowing isn't taxable, so you've got your cake free of income tax. You'll have to pay interest on the loan, but you're essentially paying it to yourself (and you can borrow that, too.) A scheme this simple probably shouldn't work if detected, due to rules against abuses of "private foundations." But tax shelter promoters claim to have found ways around those restrictions, by getting public charities, hospitals, colleges and universities, pension plans, and even local governments and Indian tribes into the act. In recent years, many such institutions have accepted payoffs from tax shelter promoters to allow their tax-exempt status to be so exploited.

For instance, a February 2005 report by the Permanent Subcommittee on Investigations of the Senate Homeland Security and Governmental Affairs Committee found that "charitable organizations, including the Los Angeles Department of Fire and Police Pensions and Austin Fire Fighters Relief and Retirement Fund, participated as counter parties in a highly questionable tax shelter . . . developed and promoted by KPMG . . . The Los Angeles pension fund, for example, . . . participated in 28 [of these] transactions over 3 years, re-sold 'donated' stock to 11 of the original 'donors,' and obtained $5.9 million in exchange, while the 'donors' themselves attempted to shelter from taxation many millions of dollars in S-Corporation income earned during the period in which the pension funds held the shares."

In fact, IRS Commissioner Mark Everson told the Senate Finance Committee in June of 2004 that almost half of the 31 highly abusive tax shelters that the IRS has recently targeted involve the participation of tax-exempt entities.

This winter, the IRS arrested billionaire Walter Anderson and charged him with evading taxes on more than $450 million in income from 1995 through 1999. Besides illustrating how preposterously long it can take the IRS to catch cheaters, Anderson's alleged tax evasion—the largest ever charged to an individual—provides a litany of tax-evasion techniques.

In 1999, for example, Anderson reported total income of $67,939 and paid income tax of only $494. The IRS says his actual income that year was $126 million. According to the IRS, Anderson set up a network of offshore corporations, sometimes under assumed names, to hide his ownership of three telecommunications companies and cover up hundreds of millions of dollars in earnings. He "donated" artworks worth millions of dollars to his private charitable foundation, yet kept the art on the walls of his house. He claimed to live in no-income-tax Florida to avoid income taxes in the District of Columbia, although at other times he asserted that he was a citizen of the Dominican Republic. "Mr. Anderson ran the table when it came to violating the tax laws," said Mark W. Everson, the current IRS head.

These well-publicized cases where the IRS has been able to crack down on certain shelters and tax cheats are edifying. But are they just the tip of an iceberg of tax evasion and avoidance that goes undetected? Or put another way, is the tax-shelter problem worse today than in the past?

In late March of this year, I posed this question to my friend Sheldon Cohen, the former IRS commissioner. His first reaction was to laugh. "Is that your whole answer," I asked. He chuckled again and went on: "Yes, of course, the problem is worse, much worse than it used to be. The enforcement is now more lax and the audit rate lower than it has ever been in the 53 years I have practiced."

How much is all this aggressive tax sheltering and evasion by high-income people costing honest American taxpayers? The truth is, nobody, including the IRS, knows. But Tax Justice Network's data suggest that the U.S. may be losing upwards of $60 billion a year in personal income taxes due to offshore investment accounts alone. The IRS just settled 1,165 cases involving a single tax shelter for $3.2 billion—an average of $1.7 million per tax avoider. All evidence points to a total cost that is staggering.

"Is it the right time to be migrating a corporation's headquarters to an offshore location? We are working through a lot of companies who feel that it is, that just the improvement on earnings is powerful enough that maybe the patriotism issue needs to take a back seat to that."
    —*Ernst & Young Webcast advising its corporate clients to shelter their profits from U.S. taxes by reincorporating in Bermuda—issued in the fall of 2001 soon after the 9/11 terrorist attacks*

"My father said all businessmen are S.O.B.s but I didn't believe it until now."
    —*John F. Kennedy,* The New York Times, *April 23, 1962*

Corporate shelters

Big corporations have an advantage over people in sheltering their income from tax. First of all, of course, they have tremendous lobbying power in Congress. So they can get special tax concessions enacted that ordinary citizens never could. In addition, unlike individuals, corporations are allowed to break themselves into pieces on paper and treat completely phony, non-existent trans-actions among those pieces as if they really happened. Because large corporations typically operate in many jurisdictions through multiple subsidiaries, they have lots of opportunities to move profits away from where they're actually earned and into places where they're not taxed.

Corporate America, outside of a few industries like oil, was a bit slow to get into the tax-avoidance game. That's why as recently as the 1950s, corporate taxes paid for about a third of the federal government. Indeed, in the early sixties, much of Big Business actually opposed the Kennedy Administration's "investment tax credit" as an unwise interference in the marketplace. But by the time that loophole had been repealed in 1969 on grounds of cost and general uselessness, big American companies had gotten a taste of tax dodging and wanted more.

President Nixon was happy to oblige, with expanded depreciation write-offs, tax breaks for exporters, and a number of other giveaways. There was a brief tax reform moment in 1976, but it was soon followed by the "supply-side" period that began in 1978 and continued through 1981. Ronald Reagan in his first term was particularly devoted to loopholes. By his second term, however, Reagan (or at least his staff) had come to his senses, and presided over the 1986 Tax Reform Act, which repealed most of the 1981-enacted tax breaks, along with many others, in exchange for lower tax rates.

But tax reform didn't last. Due to enacted loopholes, new tax-dodging schemes and insufficient enforcement, corporate tax sheltering has run amuck. Some of the shelters that corporations use are identical to the tax-avoiding schemes that wealthy people engage in. But corporations can do much more.

For example, a company may make products in one place and sell them in others. If the place it makes the products has low taxes, it may charge its selling subsidiaries, on paper, a lot for the products. That means high profits in the low tax country where the products are made, and low or no profits in the places where the products are sold. Conversely, if the place products are made has the high taxes, then the company will "sell" its products cheaply to its selling subsidiaries, and shift profits to the places where the products are sold.

Or a company may borrow from one of its subsidiaries in a low-tax place. The interest will be deductible against income that would otherwise be taxable in a higher-tax place, and taxed little, if at all by the low-tax place.

Or a company may have a very valuable asset, such as a trade name. If it transfers the ownership of that name to a low-tax place and then charges its taxable operations large royalties to use the name, it can avoid huge amounts in taxes.

One of the more blatant corporate tax shelter schemes that we know about involves a foreign company, the Yukos Oil Company, until recently Russia's biggest oil producer. After the break-up of the Soviet Union, many of Russia's previously state-owned businesses were transferred into private hands, typically at bargain basement prices. Some of the new owners became instant billionaires, and their corruption didn't stop there.

The new Russian tax code was drafted with the help of major American accounting firms, and was, on its face, as full of holes as Swiss cheese. One oddity of the Russian corporate income tax is that its revenues are dedicated to the Russian republics (the rough equivalent of our states), and those republics are authorized to give tax "incentives" to corporations, ostensibly to encourage economic development.

The republics where Yukos pumped and refined its oil weren't about to offer Yukos tax breaks. After all, they didn't need to. They already had the oil and the refineries trapped within their boundaries. But on the advice of its accountants, who included PricewaterhouseCoopers, Ernst & Young, and KPMG, Yukos found what it thought was a way around that problem. Yukos went to one of the Russian republics, Mordovia, and sought a tax break for its oil profits. This probably seemed pretty weird at first to Mordovian officials. After all, Mordovia's official Web site notes:

"There are no large deposits of natural resources except building materials on the territory of Mordovia. However. . . there are some parts of the Moksha, the Vad and the Sura rivers with deposits of the unique type of resources that is stained oak."

One can imagine the conversation between Yukos and Mordovian officials going something like this:

Yukos: We'd like a tax exemption for our Mordovian oil profits.
Mordovia: But you don't have any oil profits here in Mordovia.
Y: Maybe not yet, but we will soon.
M: What's in it for us?
Y: We'll make it worth your while.
M: And if we say no?
Y: Don't even ask.

Once Yukos got its tax exemption in Mordovia it simply transferred its profits, on paper, to that republic, and slashed its Russian income taxes down to near zero.

Unfortunately for Yukos, its thuggish billionaire chief executive, Mikail Khodorkovsky, decided to get involved in Russian politics and television. Russian President Vladimir Putin didn't like the competition and charged Khodorkovsky and Yukos with billions of dollars in tax evasion. Although the Russian tax authorities had previously ignored this misbehavior, and the Russian tax code was vague at best, it wasn't a hard case to make.

Yukos's inside-Russia tax shelter was particularly crude, but American companies do much the same thing inside the United States to avoid their state income taxes, with only a patina of added sophistication. Toys "R" Us, for example, transferred the ownership of its trade name to Delaware, which doesn't tax royalties, and then charged its stores around the country hefty fees to use the name. From 2001 through 2003, Toys "R" Us paid no state income tax on its $549 million in reported pretax U.S. profits. Similarly, many Wisconsin banks have avoided taxes by transferring ownership of their income-producing loans to subsidiaries located in Nevada, which has no income tax. Texas-based corporations such as Dell and SBC Communications have shifted the nominal ownership of their companies to partnerships located in Delaware to avoid Texas income taxes. And on and on.

This February, Citizens for Tax Justice released a study of the state income taxes of 252 of America's largest and most profitable corporations. We found that from 2001 to 2003, these companies avoided paying state income taxes on almost two-thirds of their U.S. profits—at a cost to state governments of $42 billion. Overall, corporate state tax avoidance has led to a 40% drop in state corporate income tax collections as a share of the economy from 1989 to 2003.

Shifting profits to no-tax states is just the intramural version of the much larger international tax sheltering that America's big corporations also engage in. The infamous Enron, which paid no federal income tax at all in four of five years from 1996 through 2000, had 881 subsidiaries in foreign tax-haven countries, 692 of them in the Cayman Islands alone, which it used for both tax evasion and financial shenanigans. Halliburton has hundreds of such offshore entities. Famous American logos, such as Ford and Coca Cola, are now being held by offshore affiliates in the Cayman Islands, in an international version of Toys "R" Us's state tax dodge. Most other big corporations have tax-haven subsidiaries, too, all for the purpose of hiding profits from tax.

To be sure, there are some rules against companies shifting otherwise taxable profits out of the U.S. and into tax-haven countries. Indeed, a major section of the tax code, called "Subpart F," is devoted to curbing such behavior. These rules are full of loopholes, hard to enforce and in need of reform, but they do have some salutary effect. In fact, the reason that Ernst & Young advised its corporate clients in the fall of 2001 to renounce their U.S. citizenship and reincorporate in Bermuda was that it would help get around these restrictions, since the Subpart F rules are harder to enforce or don't apply to "foreign" companies. Some of the tax schemes that multinational corporations engage in look downright wacky on their face, but they're very lucrative. For example, one of our biggest banks, Wachovia, used a leasing tax shelter in which it pretended to own a German town's sewer system. That strange scheme allowed Wachovia to eliminate all of its U.S. federal income taxes in 2002.

The list of complicated corporate tax avoidance activities is almost endless, but the effects on federal corporate tax collections are easy to understand.

When Citizens for Tax Justice examined the federal taxes of 275 of the largest U.S. corporations last September, we found that in 2003 these companies, on average, paid only 17.3% of their U.S. profits in federal income taxes—less than half the 35% rate that the tax code purportedly requires. From 2001 to 2003, 82 of the 275 corporations enjoyed at least one year in which they paid nothing at all in federal income tax, despite pretax U.S. profits in those no-tax years totaling $102 billion.

In 1965, federal and state corporate income taxes in the U.S. equaled 4.0% of our Gross Domestic Product (GDP) much more than the 2.4% average in the other major developed countries. By 2001, the latest year available for international statistics, corporate taxes in those other countries had risen to 3.2% of GDP. But American corporate taxes in 2003 had plummeted to only 1.6% of GDP. (European countries are becoming increasingly worried, however, about growing corporate tax sheltering in their jurisdictions, too.)

The bottom line is this: Due to enacted corporate tax breaks, rate reductions, and tax sheltering, U.S. corporate tax collections at the federal level alone have fallen from 4.8% of the gross domestic product in the 1950s to only 1.6% in 2004—a drop of two-thirds. To put that in perspective, if corporations paid the same effective tax rate now that they paid in the 1950s, corporate tax payments to the U.S. Treasury would be $380 billion a year higher than they actually are.

Some of that decline in federal corporate tax payments since the 1950s reflects a drop in the corporate tax rate from 52% to 35%. So cracking down on corporate tax evasion and tax sheltering wouldn't restore all of the lost revenue. But it would be a major step toward reducing the budget deficit, maintaining essential government services and protecting honest taxpayers.

> "I have not seen any material decrease in the amount of tax shelter activity. It is not as public. It is done quieter."
> — *"Mr. ABC," an IRS confidential informant who provided tax fraud involving major Wall Street firms, testifying at the Senate Finance Committee's Tax Gap Hearing, July 2004.*

"Yeah, they can pick out [a single dubious shelter] and say,
'We're putting a hell of an emphasis on this.' But will they do it
the next time? Will they do it consistently? Do they have the
manpower? Because the bad guys get it. They will behave
according to the enforcement they see."
                    — *Former IRS Commissioner Sheldon Cohen*
                    The Washington Post, *March 25, 2005*

Solutions

Lately, the IRS has gotten a lot of publicity for its crackdown on some
particularly egregious tax evasion activities, including the Walter Anderson case and the so-called "Son of BOSS" tax dodge—one of the many
complicated shelters marketed by the big accounting firms. President
Bush brags in his latest budget proposal that he's proposing a big increase in IRS enforcement resources. The accounting firms claim that
they're making so much money helping corporations comply with the
Sarbanes-Oxley Enron-inspired corporate-governance reforms that
they've sworn off marketing tax shelters.

So have we turned the corner on combating tax evasion by corporations and the wealthy? Hardly.

The majority of us who pay our taxes honestly have the right to be
assured that others do so, too. So it's disheartening how severely the
IRS's ability to curb tax sheltering and evasion—or even to know how
much is occurring—has been reduced over the past decade by Congress.
Consider:

* From 1994 to 2005, the overall IRS budget has been slashed by more
  than a fifth, both as a share of the economy and in terms of the number
  of IRS employees compared to the total U.S. population.

* In the enforcement area, the cutbacks have been even more severe.
  Last summer, the Inspector General for Tax Administration
  reported that the IRS's "enforcement staff declined from 25,000
  at the beginning of FY 1996 to 16,000 at the end of FY 2003, a
  36% decrease."

* IRS audit rates, of both businesses and individuals, declined
  precipitously, especially for upper-income tax returns. In 1996,

the IRS audited 210,000 returns of people reporting more than $100,000 in income. By 2001, the number had fallen to only 92,000—even as the number of returns with incomes above $100,000 jumped by 80%.

- In the mid-1990s, Republicans in Congress, probably at the behest of their allies and contributors in the tax-cheating business, even prohibited the IRS from doing any research on tax evasion.

Very recently, the IRS has finally been permitted to do some limited research on tax evasion (the preliminary results have just been released). Audit rates have begun to climb again, but they're still well below where they were a decade ago. Although Bush's latest budget would move a small portion of the IRS's resources away from taxpayer assistance and into enforcement, total enforcement outlays would still be no higher than in 2004 as a share of the economy, and the enforcement staff would remain more than a third below what it was a decade ago, despite the explosion in aggressive tax shelters and outright fraud since then.

Many of our political leaders in the White House and Congress are so enamored with the idea of low taxes—at least for corporations and the wealthy—that they seem to perceive allowing tax evasion as just a backdoor tax cut.

On the plus side, honest taxpayers do have a few prominent allies in the fight against tax cheating. Sen. Carl Levin (D-Mich.) has been instrumental in exposing some of the worst tax-sheltering activities by the big accounting firms. Sen. Byron Dorgan (D-N.D.) has fought against corporate offshore sheltering for decades. Senate Finance Committee Chairman Charles Grassley (R-Iowa) has held some excellent hearings on tax evasion and even sponsored legislation to curb cheating a bit— although so far Grassley has rather missed the point of reform, by insisting on devoting the revenues from his limited reform measures to opening new loopholes.

But much more typical in our current Congress are people like House Majority Leader Tom Delay (R-Tex.), who, among other things, condemns attempts to force tax havens to disclose the identities of Americans engaged in illegal offshore tax dodging as "assaults on financial privacy." As Sheldon Cohen points out, "You would have to go back to

the early 1950s to find a time when the IRS has had such low morale and support on the Hill."

As for the accounting firms, well, as Mr. ABC notes, they've definitely been embarrassed into becoming "quieter" rather than crow-
ing about their tax sheltering business. But have they really stopped
helping clients shelter their income from taxes? Have they closed
down their tax haven offices in Gibraltar and the Cayman Islands?
Don't bet on it.

If we really want to make serious progress against tax evasion,
we need to do a lot of things.

We need international cooperation to force comprehensive sharing
of information among countries, especially from tax havens. The
tax cheaters lobby and its backers are especially afraid of this kind
of reform, because offshore hiding is at the heart of many tax evasion schemes. Many foreign governments would welcome a coop-
erative crackdown on international bank secrecy—it was the Bush
Administration that pulled the plug on such cooperation when it
took office in 2001.

We need stiff fines on tax-exempt entities, including charities, pension plans, and local governments, that cooperate with tax shelter
schemes. Right now, the IRS's only weapon is to take away a charity's
tax exemption, a punishment so severe that the IRS almost never dares
impose it.

We need to frighten the lawyers and accountants with monetary
penalties for abusive behavior, so that they stop selling and blessing tax sheltering behavior.

We need to force tax lawyers to file their often bogus shelter-bless-
ing opinion letters with the IRS, so that schemes that rely on non-detec-
tion and playing the audit lottery will get scrutinized.

We need to fix the loopholes in our anti-tax-haven laws and expand
the court-made rule that tax deductions must have some real economic
substance. A good start would be to repeal the new multinational loopholes adopted by Congress last year, and instead adopt the anti-avoid-
ance provisions that the Senate approved but were dropped at the insis-
tence of the House and the tax avoidance lobby.

All of these and other changes are important. But none of them will
do the trick unless we have enough tax police to use the disclosure and
enforce the laws. So the most essential step that needs to be taken is

simply to give the IRS more resources. Just to return to the staffing levels of a decade ago would require a 50% increase in the IRS enforcement budget. Given the increase in sheltering since then, phasing in a doubling of the resources devoted to tax enforcement would not be an unreasonable goal. Fortunately, we don't have to worry about the cost. On the contrary, increasing the IRS budget is one kind of government spending that actually increases revenues.

The stakes are very high and the forces in favor of tax evasion and avoidance are well-financed and politically connected. Honest taxpayers won't win this fight until we wake up to the fact that it's our money the tax cheats are stealing—and then demand that our lawmakers do something about it.

CHAPTER 5

Closing the international tax gap

by Joseph Guttentag and Reuven Avi-Yonah[1]

In July of 1999, the Justice Department entered into a plea bargain with one John M. Mathewson of San Antonio, Texas. Mr. Mathewson was accused of money laundering through the Guardian Bank and Trust Co. Ltd., a Cayman Islands bank. Mr. Mathewson was chairman and controlling shareholder of Guardian, and in that capacity had access to information on its depositors. In return for a reduced sentence, Mr. Mathewson turned over the names of the persons who had accounts at Guardian. The result was an eye-opener: The majority of the accounts were beneficially owned by U.S. citizens, and the reason they used a Caymans bank had nothing to do with laundering funds earned in criminal activities. Instead, the accounts were in the Caymans for the purpose of evading federal income taxes on income earned legally, relying on the Caymans' lack of an income tax and promise of bank secrecy. The IRS ultimately settled 1,165 cases with the individual taxpayers for a total collection of $3.2 billion—an average of $1.7 million per taxpayer (Massey 1999 and Blum 2005).

Guardian's U.S. clients relied on four simple realities. First, in today's world, anyone can open a bank account in the Caymans for a minimal fee over the Internet, without leaving the comfort of their home. Second, the account can be opened in the name of a Caymans corporation, which can likewise be set up long-distance for minimal transaction costs (as evident from any perusal of the back pages of *The Economist* magazine, where law firms advertising such services abound). Third, money can be transferred into the account electronically from the United States or from abroad, and in most cases there would not be any reporting of such transactions to tax authorities. Finally, the funds in the Caymans account can then be used for investments in the United States and in other high tax jurisdictions, and there would generally be no withholding taxes on the resulting investment income, no Caymans taxes, and no information on the true identity of the holder available to the IRS or any other tax authority (Blum 2005). Significantly, other than the use of the Caymans, both the underlying funds that were deposited in the Guardian accounts, and the investment income, were generally purely domestic transactions, and the tax evaded was U.S. income tax on U.S. source income beneficially owned by U.S. residents.

The ability to use the Caymans and other offshore tax havens to evade income taxes is a relatively recent phenomenon. Since about 1980 there has been a dramatic lowering of both legal and technological barriers to the movement of capital, goods, and services. As countries have relaxed their tariffs and capital controls, much of the world economy has shifted from goods to services, and electronic means of delivering services and transferring funds have developed. At the same time, the tools used by tax administrations to combat tax evasion have not changed significantly: Most tax administrations are limited to enforcing taxes within their jurisdiction, and for international transactions, can only rely on outdated mechanisms like exchange of information under tax treaties with other high-tax countries, which are unavailing for income earned through tax haven corporations. Simply put, we have the technology that enables people to conduct their affairs without regard to national borders and without transparency, while restricting tax collectors to geographic borders, that are meaningless in today's world.

This chapter focuses on the problem of closing the "international tax gap," defined as the portion of taxes owed but not collected from U.S. taxpayers when an international connection of some type hinders the IRS. For example, a U.S. business owner selling goods abroad over the Internet can direct her foreign correspondent to deposit the sale proceeds in a Swiss bank account. Or a U.S. resident (like the Guardian depositors) can shift funds to a Caymans corporation and the corporation can lend these funds back to the United States and earn interest income. In neither case will there be withholding or automatic information reporting to the IRS, and as a result, it is unlikely that the IRS will be able to collect the tax due.

The size of the international tax gap

The Unites States legitimately boasts one on the world's higher compliance rates for tax collections. However, most of the taxes collected by the IRS are from income that is subject either to withholding at the source (e.g., wages) or to automatic information reporting to the IRS by financial institutions (e.g., interest or dividends from U.S. payors). The IRS has recently estimated that in 2001 there was a total "tax gap" (i.e., a difference between the taxes it collected and the taxes it should have collected under existing law) of between $312 and $353 billion, or about 16% of total taxes owed (IRS 2005). A large portion of this gap results from income that is subject to neither withholding nor information reporting, such as most income of small businesses and income earned from foreign payors. For these types of income, the compliance rate falls from over 90% to under 70% (Aaron and Slemrod 2004).

No one, including the IRS, has a good estimate of the size of the international tax gap. This is not surprising given that the activities involved are illegal, but one can make an educated guess based on a few publicly available numbers. In 2003, the Boston Consulting Group estimated that the total holdings of cash deposits and listed securities by high net worth individuals in the world were $38 trillion, and that of these, $16.2 trillion were held by residents of North America. Out of these $16.2 trillion, "less than" 10% was held offshore (as compared with, for example, 20-30% offshore for Europe and 50-70% offshore for Latin America and the Middle East) (Dyer, De Juniac, Holley, and Aerni 2004).

If one translates this estimate into approximately $1.5 trillion held offshore by U.S. residents, and if one assumes that the amount held offshore earns 10% annually, the international component of the tax gap would be the tax on $150 billion a year, or about $50 billion. This figure is in the mid-range of estimates of the international tax gap in 2002 by former IRS Commissioner Charles O. Rossotti ($40 billion) and by IRS consultant Jack Blum ($70 billion) (Sullivan 2004). As an order of magnitude, an estimate of $50 billion for the total international tax gap (for each tax year) appears congruent with the $3.2 billion actual recovery by the IRS from a single Cayman bank (for multiple tax years).

This estimate suggests that the international tax gap (i.e., *illegal* tax evasion by mostly *individual* U.S. taxpayers through cross-border activities) may be significantly greater than the total *corporate* tax gap, i.e., the underpayment of corporate taxes due to tax shelters, transfer pricing, and other tax avoidance activities, which the IRS has estimated at about $29.9 billion for 2001 (IRS 2005). And yet, as we will discuss below, the IRS expends far more resources on the corporate tax gap than on the international tax gap.

Why the international tax gap is a problem

Why should we care about the international tax gap? When the Organization for Economic Cooperation and Development (OECD) began its crackdown on tax havens in 1998, Dan Mitchell of the Heritage Foundation criticized it as a group of bloated welfare states ganging up as a cartel to quash the small, defenseless Caribbean islands that depend on offshore banking activities for their livelihood. The tax havens, it was argued, are needed to protect the property of residents of non-democratic countries from confiscation by tyrants. And the availability of low-or no-tax offshore centers serves as a salutary check on the tendency of rich country governments to increase taxes (Center for Freedom and Prosperity 2001).

However, even thoughtful supporters of tax competition like Julie Roin acknowledge that this argument is problematic when it is applied to illegal tax evasion by citizens of democratic countries (Roin 2001). After all, the desirable size of the public sector in those countries, including the United States, is the key political issue of our times, which is fought and re-fought every few years at the ballot box. Once the citizens have determined by their votes what mix of government programs they would like to pay for through their taxes, it seems perverse to argue that some of them can then legitimately opt out of participation in the process by evading the law and stashing their income overseas, away from the reach of the tax collector. After all, those citizens do not actually move to the offshore tax havens, thereby subjecting themselves to a much lower quantity and quality of government services. Instead, they stay at home and continue to enjoy the level of services provided by the rich country government, but refuse to pay their fair share of the cost (for elaboration, see Avi-Yonah 2000).

It is important to distinguish such illegal tax evasion activities by individual residents of high-tax countries from tax competition.[2] Tax competition is healthy, for example, where it increases government efficiency and the development of sound tax policies that maximize economic development while financing necessary government programs. In this way, tax competition reduces the tax burden.

None of the steps taken by the OECD, nor the ones proposed below, involve forcing the tax havens to collect taxes for OECD member countries. Rather, they involve cooperation in exchange for information, similar to what is already done voluntarily in other contexts that require such cooperation (such as the fight against international terrorism and drug cartels). Otherwise, all the suggested steps can be taken unilaterally by OECD members without discrimination and without harming the sovereignty of the tax havens.

The United States is currently facing significant budget deficits that are likely to increase as costs of entitlement programs go up. These deficits are increasing daily as a result of the ongoing "war on terror" and natural disasters like Hurricanes Katrina and Rita. Closing the tax gap by better enforcing current law is one deficit cutting measure on which Republicans and Democrats may be able to agree (see, e.g., Committee for Economic Development (2005), a bipartisan group). If the United States could collect an additional $300 billion per year (the total estimated tax gap), this would go a long way to reduce the deficit; and even a significantly lower number (presumably there will always be a tax gap) would be helpful under current conditions.

Closing or reducing the tax gap would have an effect beyond the revenue involved. A large part of the current unpopularity of the income tax has resulted from the perception that "only the little people pay taxes." If the United States can improve its collections from the rich, everyone will feel better about paying their fair share. This would ease some of the pressure from the income tax and enable a debate about replacing it with another kind of tax in a less acrimonious atmosphere. Taxpayers should not be forced to adopt a different kind of tax system because of the unwillingness (not inability) to enforce existing law, nor should taxpayers decide for themselves how much tax they would like to pay by using the loopholes in existing law to their benefit (Committee for Economic Development 2005).

Solutions to the international tax gap

Following are five steps that can be taken on a bipartisan basis to help close the international tax gap:

1. Increased IRS enforcement

It is well known that the IRS has in recent years faced an increased workload with diminished resources. From 1992 to 2001, the IRS "full-time equivalent" staff decreased by about 20,000 positions. This trend has been reversed more recently, but as former IRS Commissioner Rossotti has written, the increase is not enough to keep up with the increase in complexity of the tax system and the size of the economy (Rossotti 2004). In recent years, Congress has repeatedly increased the complexity of U.S. tax law without adding funding to the IRS. Bipartisan groups like the Committee for Economic Development (CED) have recently called for more resources and political support to be given to the IRS (CED 2005).

Decreased resources have forced the IRS to focus its attention on certain areas and neglect others, and predictably, the areas receiving the most attention have been those in the political limelight, such as the Earned Income Tax Credit (EITC) (under pressure from Republicans) and corporate tax shelters (under pressure from Democrats). However, these are not necessarily the areas likely to generate the most "bang for the buck" in terms of closing the tax gap. EITC fraud involves small amounts, and corporate tax shelters are very difficult to audit and have frequently been upheld by courts upon review. While the United States should continue its effort to combat corporate tax shelters, increased international enforcement could be even more efficient in eliminating the tax gap.

The IRS should dedicate more resources to attempting to close the international tax gap. In particular, the IRS should give more priority, and be given more resources, to audit compliance with existing laws requiring U.S. taxpayers to report ownership of foreign bank accounts and stock in foreign corporations. Moreover, the IRS should focus on auditing businesses relying on e-commerce in overseas transactions, which are particularly susceptible to abuse. If the Mathewson case is any indication, such increased attention may generate many dollars in tax revenue for every dollar spent on enforcement.[3]

2. Bilateral information exchange

The United States currently has bilateral information exchange agreements with several tax haven jurisdictions. However, most of the existing agreements are restricted only to criminal matters. Criminal matters are a very small part of overall tax collections, and pose very difficult evidentiary issues in the international context. Moreover, the agreements sometimes require the subject matter to be criminal in both the United States and the tax haven, which would never be the case for pure tax evasion. In addition, they typically require the United States to make a specific request relating to particular individuals, and they also typically do not override bank secrecy provisions in tax haven laws. These limitations mean that existing tax information exchange agreements, while helpful and important in some cases, are of limited value in closing the overall international tax gap.

The OECD has recently modified Article 26 (Exchange of Information) in its model income tax treaty, and has adopted a model Tax Information Exchange Agreement (TIEA), both of which are intended to address all of these problems. Under the new Article 26 and model TIEA, exchange of information is automatic (rather than just by request), relates to civil as well as criminal tax liabilities, does not require "dual criminality" or suspicion of a crime other than tax evasion, and overrides bank secrecy provisions in domestic laws. The United States should renegotiate its existing tax treaties and exchange of information agreements to incorporate all the changes made by the OECD in its model treaty and TIEA.

Below is a discussion of the steps needed to induce tax haven jurisdictions to negotiate such agreements with the United States. For other jurisdictions that are not tax havens, the inducement is the information they can obtain from the United States on their own residents. To ensure such information is available, the Treasury should finalize regulations proposed by the Clinton Administration that require U.S. banks and financial institutions to collect information on interest payments made to overseas jurisdictions when the interest itself is exempt from withholding under the portfolio interest exemption (Blum 2005). The Treasury has recently proposed to limit such regulations to 16 designated countries, but as Blum writes, there is no legitimate privacy or other reason to impose such limitations. The banks should collect all the information, and the Treasury should use its existing authority not to exchange it in situations in which it might be misused by non-democratic foreign governments (e.g., when freedom fighters use U.S. bank accounts).

3. Cooperation with the OECD

Current Treasury policy, possibly a reflection of broader foreign policies, is to focus on bilateral agreements to obtain needed information exchange cooperation. However, the OECD has been at the forefront of persuading tax haven jurisdictions to cooperate with information exchange, and is an organization that the United States had traditionally played a leading role in and whose work benefits both governments and the private sector. The United States should cooperate with the OECD and other appropriate international and regional organizations in their efforts to improve information exchange and, in particular, to persuade the tax havens of the world to enter into bilateral information exchange agreements based on the OECD model. The OECD has made significant progress since it began focusing on this issue in 1998, but more needs to be done, both on persuading laggard jurisdictions to cooperate and on increasing the level of information exchange available from cooperating jurisdictions.

4. Incentives to tax havens

The United States should adopt a carrot-and-stick approach to tax havens in order to provide incentives to cooperate with information exchange. In particular, the United States and other donor countries, as well as multilateral and regional organizations, should increase aid of a type that would enable tax havens to shift their economies from reliance on the offshore sector to other sources of income.

The common perception that the benefits of being a tax haven flow primarily to residents of the tax haven is misguided. The financial benefits of tax haven operations, while funding a minimal level of government services, often flow primarily to professionals providing banking and legal services, many of whom (like Mr. Mathewson) live in rich countries, rather than to the often needy residents of the tax havens. Thus, with some transitional support, most tax havens would likely see the welfare of their own residents improve as they wean themselves from dependence on the offshore sector.

5. Sanctions on non-cooperating tax havens

In the case of non-cooperating tax havens, the U.S. Treasury should use its existing authority to prospectively deny the benefits of the portfolio interest exemption to countries that do not provide adequate exchange of information.[4] This step is necessary to prevent non-cooperating tax havens from aiding U.S. residents to evade U.S. income tax.

A principal problem of dealing with tax havens is that if even a few of them do not cooperate with information exchange, tax evaders are likely to shift their funds there from cooperating jurisdictions, thereby rewarding the non-cooperating ones and deterring others from cooperation. Thus, some jurisdictions have advertised their refusal to cooperate with the OECD efforts.

However, if the political will existed, the tax haven problem could easily be resolved by the rich countries through their own action. The key observation here is that funds cannot remain in tax havens and be productive; they must be reinvested into the rich and stable economies of the world (which is why some laundered funds that need to remain in the havens earn a negative interest rate). If the rich countries could agree, they could eliminate the tax havens' harmful activities overnight by, for example, refusing to allow deductions for payments to designated non-cooperating tax havens or restricting the ability of financial institutions to provide services with respect to tax haven operations.

The financial services industry will no doubt lobby hard against such a step on the grounds that it will induce investors to shift funds to another OECD member country. However, the European Union and Japan have both committed to taxing their residents on foreign-source interest income. The EU Savings Directive, in particular, requires all EU members to cooperate in exchange of information or impose a withholding tax on interest paid to EU residents (EU 2003). Both the EU and Japan would like to extend this treatment to income from the United States. Thus, this would seem an appropriate moment to cooperate with other OECD member countries by imposing a withholding tax on payments to tax havens that cannot be induced to cooperate in exchange of information, without triggering a flow of capital out of the United States.

Conclusion

The international tax gap is a significant component of the overall tax gap and may in fact be larger than some components that have attracted more public and IRS attention, like corporate tax shelters or EITC fraud. In order to maintain any kind of tax system, the U.S. public needs to be confident that current law can be enforced and that tax evasion will be caught and prosecuted. Bipartisan support is needed for taking the steps identified above to close the international tax gap. These steps offer the potential of raising additional revenue without raising taxes, and of leveling the playing field between ordinary Americans who pay their fair share of taxes and others who do not.

Endnotes

1.   We would like to thank Henry Aaron, Max Sawicky, Eric Toder, and Philip West for their extremely valuable comments on earlier versions of this chapter. Any remaining errors are our responsibility.

2.   Tax competition is the use by governments (localities, states, or nations) of preferential tax treatment—reduced rates or some sort of deduction, credit, or exclusion—to attract taxable activity to their jurisdictions.

3.   For example, transfers by U.S. banks to foreign banks, such as occurred in the Mathewson case, generate bank records which can be audited by the IRS. Similar records may not exist for transfers from foreign banks or non-bank networks (e.g., the *hawala* trust-based network). These types of transfers are also used by terrorists and it would be advisable to use the well-developed expertise of the IRS to combat both tax evasion and terrorist financing activities.

Similarly, more use can be made of credit card records and other data mining techniques to establish which U.S. taxpayers have foreign accounts that they have not disclosed (as required by current law) on their tax return.

4.   See Internal Revenue Code section 871(h)(6).

References

Aaron, Henry J. and Joel Slemrod (eds.). 2004. *The Crisis in Tax Administration*. Washington, D.C.: The Brookings Institution.

Avi-Yonah, Reuven S. 2000. Globalization, Tax Competition, and the Fiscal Crisis of the Welfare State. Cambridge: *Harvard. Law Review*. Vol. 103.

Blum, Cynthia. 2005. Sharing bank peposit information with other countries: Should tax compliance or privacy claims prevail. Florida.*Tax Review*. Vol. 6. p. 579.

Dyer, Andrew, Christian De Juniac, Bruce M. Holley, and Victor Aerni. 2004. *The Rich Return to Richer Returns: Global Wealth 2004*. Boston: Boston Consulting Group. November. http://www.bcg.com/publications/files/GW_short_Nov_04.pdf.

Center for Freedom and Prosperity. 2001. CFP declares victory, but says fight against OECD initiative is far from over. *Tax Notes Text*. pp. 95-35.

Committee for Economic Development. 2005. *A New Tax Framework: A Blueprint for Averting a Fiscal Crisis*. Washington, D.C.: CED.

European Union. 2003. Directive 2003/48/EC on Taxation of Savings.

Internal Revenue Service. 2005. *The Tax Gap*. http://www.irs.gov/pub/irs-utl/tax_gap_facts-figures.pdf

Massey, Boyd.1999. Convicted bank chairman is key to dozens of new tax haven cases. *Tax Notes Text*. pp.171-2.

Merrill Lynch. 2004. *World Wealth Report.* www.ml.com/media/18252.pdf.

Roin, Julie. 2001. Competition and evasion: Another perspective on international competition. *Georgetown Law Review.* Vol. 80, No. 543.

Rossotti, Charles O. 2004. Letter to Senators Charles Grassley and Max Baucus. March 22.

Sullivan, Martin A. 2004. U.S. citizens hide hundreds of billions in Cayman accounts. *Tax Notes.* Vol. 103, p. 956.

CHAPTER 6

Tax simplification and tax compliance: An economic perspective

by Wojciech Kopczuk

The gross tax gap in 2001—the amount of federal taxes not paid voluntarily and on time—was estimated to be between $312 billion and $353 billion, or between 15% and 16.6% of total tax liability (IRS 2005b). Clearly, enforcement of taxes in the United States is far from perfect. This chapter considers the extent to which tax law should be enforced, and analyzes the best means to improve compliance with tax law.

The main argument is that the appropriate extent of tax enforcement critically depends on the underlying tax structure. In particular, the role of complexity in the tax system as a factor influencing the size of the tax gap, as well as legal but undesirable tax avoidance, are highlighted.

Two principal implications of tax complexity are stressed here. First, complexity permits additional ways to shield income from tax and, consequently, complexity increases the overall cost of taxation.

Second, complexity increases the likelihood that taxpayers make inadvertent mistakes in calculating their tax liabilities. From this standpoint, penalties are a less appealing means of enforcement, and increasing the probability of detection becomes more costly. Hence, tax complexity undermines the effectiveness of tools at the disposal of the Internal Revenue Service.

The central objective of reform should be simplifying the tax system. Reasonable simplification can more adequately combat tax eva-

sion and avoidance than traditional enforcement measures and, at
the same time, simplification would make standard enforcement
policies more effective without increased enforcement spending.

The ideal compliance policy should target both tax avoidance
and tax evasion. While there is a legal distinction between the two,
from the economic point of view the difference is less explicit. Both
types of activity involve a loss of revenue and both involve a loss of
economic welfare.[1] The loss of revenue implies an additional economic cost because the revenue must be recouped by resorting to
further distortionary taxation.[2]

In the case of the simplest form of tax evasion, an additional loss of
welfare is due to the risk taken by the (cheating) taxpayer. In the case of
more complicated forms of purely tax-motivated financial planning, taxpayers use up real resources to shelter income. Preventing such waste
should be a leading concern in tax policy. In particular, from an efficiency point of view,[3] it does not matter whether or not the underlying
activity is legal.

The main points in this chapter are:

- While the implications of tax complexity are multi-dimensional, its
  most important consequence is the extent of opportunities for tax
  avoidance and evasion that it creates.

- By reducing tax complexity, policy makers change how responsive
  taxpayers can be to changes in taxation. Consequently, a less complex
  tax system may provide a lower marginal excess burden of taxation.[4]
  There is some evidence that this was the result of the Tax Reform
  Act (TRA) of 1986. When the tax system is less costly, enforcement
  is less important because alternative ways of collecting revenue are
  less damaging.

- Tax evasion is illegal while tax avoidance may be legal, but from the
  economic point of view, they are similarly costly and tax avoidance
  should be a higher priority target.

- Tax complexity increases the likelihood that taxpayers are non-
  compliant unintentionally. This has an important policy consequence:
  when taxpayers make honest mistakes, enforcing taxes is harder
  because it requires distinguishing between cheaters and honest-but-

confused taxpayers. Therefore, complexity reduces the effectiveness of standard enforcement tools such as detection or penalties.

• There may be positive aspects of tax avoidance (an incomplete list is in the section "Social benefits of not enforcing" on p. 127). One should consider opportunities for tax avoidance as a potential policy tool. While in most cases avoidance is undesirable, there may be circumstances when limited and judiciously designed avoidance opportunities are socially beneficial.

The plan of this chapter is as follows. In the next two sections, the basic economic approach to tax evasion and tax avoidance is presented. This is followed by a discussion of the social costs of evasion and avoidance. Subsequently, implications for the appropriate extent of enforcement and the impact of complexity are drawn. Next, for completeness, a number of arguments suggesting that tax avoidance and/or evasion can have positive social spillovers are offered. The final section of this chapter contains a discussion of enforcement and complexity in specific cases: the Earned Income Tax Credit, reliance on floors and ceilings for deductions, the role of tax preparers, and the use of phase-ins and phase-outs of tax provisions.

Preliminaries—straightforward cheating

The basic theoretical framework for tax evasion was derived by Allingham and Sandmo (1972) from the Becker model of crime (Becker 1968). This approach views tax evasion as a gamble. Some degree of risk is always present in the context of evasion, so this model captures at least one important aspect of non-compliance. It may not capture all important determinants of tax evasion, and some extensions of it will be discussed below.

In cases when tax evasion is successful, the taxpayer gains by not paying taxes. In other cases, tax evasion is uncovered by tax authorities, and the taxpayer has to pay taxes due and fines. The taxpayer compares the expected gain to the expected loss. The expected gain or loss is the size of the possible gain or loss multiplied by its probability. For instance, if 100 people each have an equal chance to win a lottery with a prize of $100, the expected gain is $1.

In the economic models, the decision whether to evade at all turns out to depend only on this comparison: if the expected gain is greater than the expected loss, the taxpayer decides to evade at least a little. How much is evaded depends on the aversion to risk, the expected gain, and the risk faced by the taxpayer.

This approach highlights a number of factors that determine whether and to what extent taxes are evaded. These are: the magnitude of potential savings (which, on the margin, is simply equal to the tax rate); the probability of getting caught; and penalties when caught. More subtly, the extent (but not the presence) of evasion depends on risk aversion, which itself may be a function of the level of income, and it may depend on the tax liability. This model therefore highlights three natural policy parameters that can affect evasion. The IRS can work harder at trying to find cheaters, it can punish them more severely, or the marginal gains from tax evasion could be reduced by imposing lower marginal tax rates. A more unorthodox enforcement measure would entail overstating the risk of getting caught, or trying to affect preferences for risk.[5] Each of these tools has associated problems.

Penalties for tax evasion have generally been low, perhaps barring relatively rare criminal cases. This is puzzling in the light of the Allingham-Sandmo model, because that approach implies that penalties are *the* preferred way of dealing with tax evasion. One would like to reduce the expected gain from cheating. Very high penalties naturally help in achieving this and, the argument goes, imposing penalties is cheap while increasing the probability of detection is not. Among various types of possible penalties, monetary fines have the advantage of recouping revenue while criminal sanctions do not. Therefore, increasing penalties that focus on fines is a natural policy response.

While this may be true in an idealized world, in practice it does not seem to be the case. There is no doubt that penalties could be increased beyond their current levels. However, one needs massive increases in penalties to make the expected gain from tax evasion negative. Under audit rates of 1% (this is approximately the audit rate nowadays, but as will be discussed later, this is not necessarily the right measure of the probability of detection), and a marginal tax rate of 35% (for the highest income taxpayers), cheating the government out of a dollar in taxes due results in an expected gain of 34.6

cents (0.99*0.35=34.6). To combat this gain and discourage a risk-averse taxpayer from pursuing any tax evasion, the expected loss should be equal to the gain. The expected loss is 0.01 times the penalty, and therefore the penalty (per dollar of cheating) should be $34.65. This is several orders of magnitude higher than current penalties. Penalties of this magnitude would certainly be extremely controversial, and they may not even be legal.

There are also reasons why very large penalties may not be desirable. For one thing, distinguishing honest mistakes from cheating is hard, and therefore in practice penalties cannot be exorbitant. Furthermore, when high penalties require criminal prosecution, they are neither easy nor cheap to implement.

The natural alternative to penalties is a higher probability of detection. Audits may take many different forms. Standard audits—direct examination of a taxpayer's return and financial records—are one example, but there are many others. Detecting misreporting early on by automatic cross-checking of taxpayer information from alternative sources, also known as document matching, is another example.

The withholding system effectively eliminates evasion of taxable income by making detection a near-absolute certainty. Nevertheless, expanding such approaches is undoubtedly costly.

The third class of policy tools is setting marginal tax rates. Low marginal tax rates may reduce the incentive to cheat on the margin, although from a theoretical point of view, the effect is ambiguous when penalties are proportional to the tax evaded, rather than income unreported (Yitzhaki 1974). Low marginal tax rates also reduce revenue collections, and therefore relying on this tool for combating tax evasion requires adjustments in the tax code elsewhere, perhaps offsetting the potential gains.

Tax avoidance

The risk in tax evasion is not beyond the taxpayer's control. In fact, sophisticated kinds of tax planning blur the line between legality and crime and therefore reduce the likelihood that the transaction will be questioned.

This discussion will not try to clearly delineate tax avoidance from tax evasion. The distinction stressed here is in terms of the cost to the taxpayer: informally speaking, activities where the ultimate tax treatment is uncertain, with the risk imperfectly controlled by tax collection agency, could be classified as evasion. Activities where costs have a different nature are avoidance. When a tax-saving scheme is illegal, it is uncertain whether a preferential tax treatment will be ultimately available, and therefore such a scheme is naturally considered evasion according to this classification. Taking advantage of tax incentives (e.g., selling and buying back the same asset in response to a temporarily reduced capital gains rate) does not involve uncertainty about the ultimate tax treatment and is considered avoidance.[6] Many kinds of real-life tax planning are likely to have elements of both.

The concept of avoidance has a number of implications within the framework that we have just discussed. First, taxpayers have a range of options: there is no single kind of tax avoidance. Second, probabilities of detection are lower than for outright tax evasion, and they may be reduced further if the taxpayer chooses to invest in protecting herself by hiring an adviser, paying for a legal opinion, or structuring the transaction appropriately. Third, each of these extra options has various kinds of costs associated with it that are not present under the simplest kind of tax evasion. One of these costs has already been mentioned: taxpayers can invest in reducing the probability of detection. In addition, there may be a fixed cost necessary in order to even attempt tax avoidance: hiring a professional may not be optional but rather a necessary condition for pursuing a particular kind of tax avoidance, and so can be the cost of having an off-shore account, a foreign subsidiary, or a charitable foundation of a future estate taxpayer. Furthermore, pursuing an avoidance strategy may require modifying real economic decisions or subjecting oneself to extra constraints (for example, a tax shelter may be illiquid).

On the other hand, combating tax avoidance is harder for tax authorities. Because taxpayers are blurring the line between legal and illegal, establishing that the behavior in question is in fact illegal requires expending resources. Auditing a single taxpayer may no longer be enough: transactions may have many participants. A court battle may ensue as a result. Tax auditors need considerable knowledge to cope with tax planning. Accordingly, their qualifications and compensation have to increase with the sophistication of those who practice avoidance strategies.

Understanding that tax avoidance adds extra costs is the key point, because the costs affect how harmful the activity is from a social point of view, and therefore how much it should be discouraged. (This issue is discussed below.)

Availability of simple tax evasion is a fact of nature—one can always cheat—but tax avoidance is not. Tax avoidance is a function of ambiguity in the tax system. This is not to say that ambiguity can always be avoided in real life. Still, what and how many avoidance opportunities are available depend on the structure of the tax system. Consider the simplest of taxes: a uniform poll tax—let us say that everybody has to pay $10,000 in taxes. There is still room for tax evasion: tax authorities have to find the taxpayer to make him pay, and there are places in the New York subway system where no authorities will venture. Making oneself hard to find is all that one can do, however, if there is a desire to cheat.

Any attempt to complicate the system will introduce extra possibilities for avoidance. For example, if we limit the tax to adults, we will have to determine who the adults are. While forging a birth certificate is illegal, it is not impossible (and neither is a decision not to induce birth on December 31st). If we limit the tax to working adults, we will have to determine the appropriate definition of working and monitor appropriately.

Any attempt to make tax liability different for different individuals will introduce incentives to respond. At various points in history there were attempts to impose taxes on the number of windows, beards, and servants. Not surprisingly, they gave rise to predictable tax anecdotes. In the 19th century, the United States had occupation-based taxes: naturally, it made it worthwhile to misrepresent one's occupation. Any modern tax system will create these kinds of incentives, but some will create more than others.

What determines the extent of such ambiguity? Stiglitz (1985) highlights three principles of tax avoidance: postponement of taxes, arbitrage across individuals subject to different marginal tax rates, and manipulation of different types of income that are taxed to different degrees. It is clear from this classification that the key factor affecting opportunities for tax avoidance is the number of options under different tax treatments.[7] What is an option is hard to specify in the abstract, perhaps partly explaining why measuring and understanding the overall cost of complexity appears so hard to do. There have been only limited attempts to formalize this issue in empirical work.

Triest (1992) recognized the importance of itemization and analyzed the labor supply responses. Kopczuk (2005) measures complexity as a fraction of income reported on the tax return that is not subject to taxation and provides a simple theoretical model justifying this measure as an adequate summary of opportunities for shifting income away from taxable form. There is a voluminous literature on behavioral responses to assorted tax provisions (Slemrod and Yitzhaki 2002 provide a recent survey).

It should be noted here that complexity need not be increased by new rules. To the contrary, if new statutes are intended to clarify the existing law or to ban particular loopholes discovered by taxpayers, they may result in the overall reduction of opportunities for tax avoidance. It could be argued, therefore, that such an extension of the tax code, if successful, in fact reduces complexity even though it adds to the tax code. The question is whether the new rule is successful in closing avoidance opportunities.

Summarizing, any differential treatment of two related economic activities gives rise to an opportunity for avoiding and, therefore, opportunities for avoidance are naturally a function of complexity in the tax code. A natural way of reducing avoidance opportunities is therefore a simplification of the tax code. To reduce complexity, such a simplification must involve reducing the number of special tax treatments. Since special tax treatment most often takes the form of tax preferences (deductions, credits, and exclusions from income), the corresponding expansion of the tax base allows for reduced rates and may have a side-effect of further reducing opportunities to avoid taxes.

In this context, it is interesting to note that this was the direction of the Tax Reform Act of 1986 (TRA). It is suggestive (though hardly definitive) to observe that the estimated tax gap in the aftermath of the TRA 86 actually declined from a bit over 18.5% in 1985 to a little bit less than 17.5% in 1988 (IRS 1996).[8] The tax gap is an estimate of tax evasion only.

Although the loss of revenue due to avoidance is much harder to compute, Gordon and Slemrod (1988) calculated that the U.S. tax system in 1983 collected no revenue from taxing capital income, in

large part due to tax arbitrage.   But when they repeated the calcula-
tions well after the TRA 86 (for 1995), they found that no longer to
be true.   They estimated that capital income tax revenue exceeded
100 billion (Gordon, Kalambokidis, and Slemrod 2004).

Cost of avoidance and evasion

Private costs
Some costs of non-compliance have already been mentioned.   Tax
evasion is a decision under risk.   As such, it reduces the taxpayer's
welfare relative to receiving the same expected amount with certainty.   At the other end of the range of tax-motivated planning
activities, cost has nothing to do with risk, but instead involves paying for advice, tax preparers, misallocating resources, and so on.
Most tax planning falls in between and involves both exposure to
risk and extra costs.

Some exposure to risk is likely to characterize transactions that fall
in the gray area between unambiguously legal tax planning and unambiguously illegal tax evasion. For example, a taxpayer may be uncertain
whether a transaction is going to be challenged and finally accepted by
the IRS, or a taxpayer may view the whole situation as negotiation with
the IRS, subject to an uncertain outcome.

Extra costs may also be associated with unambiguously illegal tax
evasion.   The benefit to the consumer of avoiding a dollar is given by
expected tax savings minus expected penalties. Taxpayers will pursue
evasion/avoidance until the marginal benefit is equal to the marginal
cost:

expected gain =
direct non-risk costs + welfare loss due to exposure to risk

(where all effects are on the margin).   Note that the loss due to extra
exposure to risk accrues to the cheating taxpayer but does not by itself
affect other individuals.   Direct costs, on the other hand, create a
real resource cost for the economy.   While it is true that in either case the marginal cost is equal to
the taxpayer's expected gain, direct costs are different in two re-
spects from the "risk exposure" category.   First, by affecting the

real side of the economy, they may have implications for tax revenue from other sources. This effect may be negative (for example, time spent shredding documents is not devoted to a taxable activity), or positive (the shredder itself is taxable, otherwise the taxpayer might buy non-taxable carrots instead).

Second, by affecting the real side of the economy and therefore relative prices, other taxpayers are affected by avoidance. From the distributional point of view, such effects may be harmful or beneficial, depending on the direction of the effect. In practice both evasion and avoidance will feature both direct costs and risk-related costs, but the composition will be different.

Although the welfare implications of spillovers due to the direct costs are ambiguous in theory, they should be deemed harmful in practice unless there is strong evidence to the contrary. Revenue implications are, if anything, negative for important kinds of costs such as time spent planning and implementing non-compliance. Hiring tax professionals, while it may contribute to higher tax revenue from taxes imposed on their incomes (depending on whether the marginal reduction in spending on other things was subject to higher or lower tax rates), corresponds to an increased demand for relatively high-skilled labor and therefore, it is likely to exacerbate rather than reduce inequality.

Concluding this discussion, both tax evasion and tax avoidance have private costs that the taxpayer compares to expected tax savings. Private costs also constitute a social welfare loss, because the gain to the taxpayer is a loss to the budget and therefore only a transfer and not a net gain to the economy. Furthermore, tax avoidance and tax evasion are equally costly (holding tax savings constant) on the margin, when only the effect on the cheating taxpayer is considered. Therefore, as a matter of economic efficiency, focusing solely on tax evasion is not warranted, and tax avoidance should be considered as an equally serious problem, even though one activity may be borderline legal and the other not. Finally, negative spillovers from tax avoidance are likely greater than spillovers from tax evasion, strengthening the case for targeting tax avoidance as a policy objective.

Inequity

The second class of costs due to tax avoidance has to do with fairness. This discussion will be confined to considerations of horizontal equity.[9]

This concept is hard to quantify (see Auerbach and Hassett 2002 for an attempt), although most have an intuition for what it means to treat equals equally.

In the context of tax evasion, horizontal equity may be compromised for two reasons. First, successful and unsuccessful evaders are treated unequally *ex post*. This is not a serious concern, both because *ex ante* they have identical welfare, and because most people would not be concerned about unfair treatment of cheaters.

Second, there is horizontal inequity between otherwise equal people who do cheat, and those who do not. The relevant question is why there is a difference in the behavior of otherwise identical individuals. There may be many reasons: different attitudes toward cheating, different access to avoidance opportunities, differences in perception of risk, or different circumstances.

The first two of these truly amount to the tax code treating individuals differently based on their tastes or occupation. Differences in perceptions may be indicative of differences in ability to understand complex economic problems, and thus may indicate that these taxpayers are not in fact "equal," even though other observable criteria (such as income) would have suggested so. Similarly, taxpayers may experience different circumstances. For example, it has been suggested that cheating taxpayers are in fact worse off (Andreoni 1992), and they treat the IRS as a sort of lender of last resort. If this were the real reason for most tax evasion and avoidance, horizontal inequity would not in fact be a valid concern. Empirical work has, however, failed to convincingly establish a relationship between tax evasion and personal circumstances, and we still lack an understanding of the determinants of compliance. It appears very likely that a lot of tax evasion is a matter of personal preference, and in that case the horizontal equity considerations should be taken seriously.

Distortionary taxation

A loss of revenue is a transfer from the government to the cheating or avoiding individual, but the social value of government's revenue and private dollars is not the same. This is because collecting taxes requires distortionary taxes, and therefore a dollar of revenue lost by the government leads to extra cost from additional taxes.[10] Because there is a difference between social valuations of government and private dollars of evaded taxes, the presence of non-compliance reduces welfare even if the private costs of evasion and avoidance are zero and horizontal equity is not a concern.

Enforcement approaches

A simple but illuminating finding about enforcement is presented in Baldry (1984). Suppose that a bit more enforcement increases the total cost of enforcement; in other words, it is costly on the margin. Then it is never optimal to eliminate all evasion. This is because the social loss from the first dollar of tax evasion is negligible, while the cost of administration is not. Given that full enforcement makes no sense (and is not even possible), the question is the best level. The usual economic answer is that the marginal cost of enforcement should be equal to its marginal benefit. Implementing that solution requires identifying the costs and benefits.

There are two costs of combating tax evasion or avoidance. First, authorities spend money on enforcement. Second, as discussed in the previous section, taxpayers who cheat face some likelihood of getting caught and penalized. Taxpayers who avoid taxes legally face other types of costs. All in all, the dollar of tax savings is not worth a full dollar to either side. What are the benefits? More tax revenue is collected.

How do costs and benefits compare? With reduced evasion or avoidance, a taxpayer loses a dollar and the government gains a dollar. If the value of this expected dollar in the government's coffers is the same as its value to the individual, there is no gain. In fact, there is likely a loss because the government pays for enforcement. As discussed in the previous section, however, these values are not the same. The expected dollar from evasion involves a risk. When taxpayers are averse to risk, the expected dollar is worth less than a certain dollar from the individual standpoint. At the same time, a government that deals with many different taxpayers is not affected by this kind of idiosyncratic risk. By pursuing enforcement the government reduces the exposure to risk and that is a good thing.

We further need to consider alternative sources of financing. Gaining a dollar of revenue reduces the need to rely on other taxes. Because other sources of revenue are distortionary, the extra burden imposed by the need to rely on alternative sources is the cost of evasion, and eliminating the need to resort to alternative revenue sources (higher taxes) is a gain. Enforcement from this perspective is therefore beneficial, and its profitable extent is limited only because it is costly (see Mayshar 1991 for an extended discussion along these lines).

Note, however, that the benefits of reducing tax evasion are especially subtle. Collecting more revenue by itself is not a benefit, because it only represents a transfer from individuals to government. It becomes beneficial only because it reduces the exposure to risk by evaders and, perhaps more appealingly, because it reduces the need for other taxes. The same applies to tax avoidance but, as argued above, avoiding misallocation of resources devoted to financing tax avoidance is more important than reducing cheating taxpayers' exposure to risk.

Administrative investment in enforcement becomes more important when the tax system is more distortionary. One way to reduce the need for costly tax enforcement is to reduce distortions. Under a more efficient tax structure, the same level of tax evasion will have a lower cost. It has been suggested that how distortionary the tax system is (in terms of the marginal cost of funds—the ancillary costs of collecting a dollar of revenue) does depend on the choice of tax structure. This point was originally suggested by Slemrod (1994), and it was analyzed in detail by Slemrod and Kopczuk (2002). The issue goes back to the previous discussion of complexity. Higher complexity induces tax avoidance and other types of substitution responses. A tax system that allows for many different types of avoidance responses is likely to cause stronger behavioral effects and therefore higher excess burden. In other words, the cost of additional revenue is higher. Shrinking the menu of tenable responses reduces the marginal excess burden of taxation, and therefore the benefits of extensive tax enforcement are lower.

Shutting down extra margins of response can be loosely summarized as expanding the tax base by eliminating preferential treatment of some types of income, deductions, and exemptions. In the context of the personal income tax, Kopczuk (2005) estimated that the elasticity of income reported on individual income tax returns[11] as well as the elasticity of taxable income falls when the tax base is broader.[12] One implication, therefore, is that the need for extensive tax enforcement was likely to be lower after the Tax Reform Act of 1986, since the tax base was broadened.

The notion that the excess burden of taxation and therefore the benefit of stronger enforcement varies with the tax base is also consistent with other findings in the taxable income literature, such as varying elasticities by itemization status (Gruber and Saez 2002), elasticities varying with the tax reform (Saez 2004), or with the source of income (Sillamaa and Veall 2001).

Without changes in the tax structure, the choice of where to put an administrative dollar becomes more critical. Assume that revenue gains from any type of reduced evasion go in the same general revenue category. Different targets for increased enforcement will have different implications for risk exposure and will have different revenue consequences. Under a more distortionary tax system more weight should be placed on the latter aspect: the types of enforcement that most increase revenue are more valuable. When the tax system is otherwise relatively efficient, the individual cost considerations become more important.

Complexity, confusion, and penalties

One of the consequences of complexity is that it makes it difficult for honest taxpayers to fulfill their obligations. When understanding the tax code is difficult, taxpayers are bound to make mistakes. The uncertainty that an honest taxpayer faces in figuring out her true tax liability may result in overpayment of taxes on average (Scotchmer and Slemrod 1989), but this source of revenue is not a net social gain because it is due to extra cost or hassle imposed on taxpayers. Liebman and Zeckhauser (2005) argue that individuals respond to complexity by ignoring the details and using heuristics instead. The revenue implications of such behavior are ambiguous.

The mix of intentional and unintentional mistakes complicates enforcement. In essence, it reduces the ability of authorities to rely on standard tools of enforcement. While it is likely true that higher penalties will result in more effort devoted to compliance, they are unlikely to eliminate mistakes altogether. In fact, if penalties are an effective tool for reducing intentional cheating, high penalties may lead to a situation where the only penalized taxpayers are the honest but confused ones. Because honest taxpayers will sometimes be penalized, penalties imply a cost that is not otherwise present.

One possible channel of taxpayer response to increased enforcement is to reduce their claims for objectively legitimate but subjectively uncertain credits and deductions, with a resulting increase in the overall tax liability. Assuming a good reason for these types of tax preferences to begin with, foregoing them is harmful, even though revenue consequences are positive. It is also likely to be horizontally inequitable, as more sophisticated taxpayers are likely to be less affected.

Another possible channel of response is to opt out of the tax system, either partially or altogether by not filing at all (see Erard and Ho 2001, for evidence of the importance of non-filing), shifting a business to the informal 'underground' sector or switching to tax bases where either uncertainty or the probability of detection is lower. These types of responses may have negative revenue implications.

The probability of detection is another leading instrument of enforcement. Taxpayer confusion due to complexity undermines the value of this approach as well. Assuming that the tax collection agency does not wish to penalize honest taxpayers, it has to attempt to establish whether cheating occurred intentionally, or whether it was an honest mistake. This adds an extra layer of costs after detection of an incorrect filing that would not be present otherwise. Furthermore, when taxpayers can claim that non-compliance was unintentional, penalties become uncertain as well (hence reducing the effective "probability of detection"), even when the agency intends to impose them, unless taxpayers are denied the right to defend themselves. When a legal battle ensues, there is also a possibility of horizontal inequity, as more-sophisticated taxpayers may do better in such circumstances.

The bottom line is that complexity makes relying on penalties a much less appealing approach to enforcement. This is so for two reasons: penalties and audits become more costly because they have to be associated with some attempt to distinguish honest taxpayers from cheaters, and they directly reduce the welfare of honest taxpayers.

Manipulating the probability of detection

Increasing the probability of detection should reduce cheating by rational taxpayers. Devoting more resources to audits would increase the probability of detection and therefore expected penalties. With no changes to the underlying tax structure and no ability to significantly increase penalties, devoting more resources to detection is the way to go if one wants to reduce non-compliance. To the extent that an examiner may be able to arrive at an informed judgment about whether a taxpayer made a mistake or was cheating intentionally, more detailed audits would also alleviate problems resulting from taxpayers' confusion. Increased auditing would also increase the probability of penalizing dishonest taxpayers who are audited and, therefore, the overall probability of being subject to penalties. The problem with direct audits is that they are costly.

Auditing is not the only way of increasing the probability of detection. Withholding and matching various sources of data by the IRS are also measures that affect detection. This more general definition of the probability of detection helps in making sense of the patterns of non-compliance. Compliance is very high in case of wages and salaries that are subject to withholding, and where the IRS can match taxpayers report to the W2 form.[13] Almost 99% of such income is reported accurately. Misreporting of business income is much harder to monitor, since no independent source of information is available. In this area there is 30% misreporting, according to the 1992 IRS estimates.

Some categories where misreporting is non-trivial are puzzling. Misreporting of alimony income and unemployment income is sizable (on the order of 20% and 10% in 2001, respectively), and the 2001 estimates also include a 6% misreporting of state income tax refunds (a much higher rate than in 1992). These categories are puzzling because verification is relatively straightforward—in the case of state refunds and unemployment it requires respective state agencies and the IRS to exchange information. In the case of alimony, a taxpayer who claims a deduction for alimony payments is required to report the Social Security number of the spouse, so matching this information should also be automatic.

The IRS has been well aware of the potential for detecting non-compliance by cross-matching various source of information, but much remains to be done. For example, Steuerle (2005a) has suggested that requiring financial intermediaries to report net capital gains rather than just total payments from sales of assets would increase compliance in this area by allowing the IRS to cross-match taxpayer's reports with those obtained from financial institutions, while simultaneously reducing compliance costs. Similarly, Steuerle (2005b) suggested that the IRS should expand reporting of charitable contributions by charities, with an ultimate objective of matching them against individual reports. Changes in the ability of the IRS to match various sources of information as well as new reporting requirements have increased the effective probability of detection without changing the number of audits. The number of audits had been declining until 2000, and it has increased in the past few years, though it still remains below historical levels. At the same time, the expanded use of cross-matching of various sources of information has contributed to the increase in the effective rate of detection of cheating for many types of income. Consequently, it is hard to judge whether the probability of detection is now higher or lower than it was in the past. Unfortunately, there are not enough estimates of the tax gap to study the relationship between its various determinants, but the overall size of the tax gap based on 2001 data does not look markedly different than it was in the past. Using the size of the tax gap as a share of revenue, the non-compliance rate was estimated to be 18.5-18.8% in 1985, 17.2-17.5% in 1988, and 16.9-17.3% in 1992 (IRS 1996) and 15.0-16.6% in 2001 (IRS 2005).[14]

Social benefits of not enforcing

It is natural to think of tax avoidance and evasion as unmitigated evils that should arise only because the cost of eradicating them is too high. There are, however, some situations when eliminating avoidance would not be desirable, even if it was possible at a low cost.

The first argument is redistributive. Increasing the extent of redistribution is costly because it requires increasing effective marginal tax rates at least for some, and therefore increasing the excess burden of taxation. A simple insight of Akerlof (1978) is that governments should rely on "tagging": they should use observable characteristics of individuals that are correlated with the need for redistribution. As shown by Kopczuk (2001), this logic applies in the context of tax avoidance: to the extent that particular types of avoidance are more likely to be pursued by low-ability individuals, an optimal redistributive policy may involve laxer enforcement in this dimension.

One example is an informal economy where the benefits are skewed toward low-income individuals (or, at least, let's assume that for the sake of the argument). Enforcing taxes in this context while compensating would-be nannies using other redistributive policies would require extra revenue and therefore increasing marginal tax rates at the top of the income distribution. Not enforcing allows for holding tax rates lower and, because of the nature of this activity, does not otherwise affect labor supply decisions of the higher income population that is not as inclined to operate in the informal economy. From this point of view, enforcement of taxes at the bottom of the distribution should be given a lower priority than at the top, although horizontal equity issues are a serious mitigating concern.

The second class of arguments has to do with diverse preferences. Perhaps its best application is tax avoidance in the context of the estate tax. It is generally believed that avoiding the estate tax is relatively easy (although see Schmalbeck 2001 for an important qualification: most avoidance strategies involve a loss of control over assets and therefore may be undesirable and costly to the taxpayer). Still, estate tax revenue is significant and taxpayers do appear to be ignoring some simple and effective avoidance strategies, such as making annual, tax-free *inter vivos* gifts.

Suppose that there are two classes of estate taxpayers. The first class includes those who have no interest in leaving an inheritance, but who save for their own benefit, either to finance future spending or to enjoy benefits derived from controlling assets. Leaving a bequest is just a side-effect of their behavior. The second group are those who save with beneficiaries in mind. Estate taxes have different consequences for the two groups: they influence decisions of the latter group but are of no consequence to the former. Imposing heavier taxation on the former group would therefore be desirable; allowing for easy tax avoidance reflects such a policy. Those who would otherwise be hurt by taxation avoid it at a low cost while those who do not care about bequests pay the tax. Other than the costs associated with implementing avoidance strategies, no extra damage is done.

As another example, the presence of tax avoidance opportunities for multi-nationals may keep them from shifting their operations abroad, while not affecting the decisions of domestic corporations.

Third, a higher efficiency cost of taxation can be beneficial in some contexts. Becker and Mulligan (2003) argue that a high deadweight loss of taxation imposes a constraint on the growth of government spending. Taking this argument seriously, a complicated tax system is a commitment device for policy makers not to spend too much or not to raise taxes. Alternatively, it may be a constraint imposed by one political group on another.

Fourth, too much auditing can backfire. Slemrod, Blumenthal, and Christian (2001) found making audits a certainty, by sending taxpayers a letter informing them that they will definitely be audited, resulted in a *reduction* in voluntary compliance by high-income taxpayers. This may seem puzzling until one realizes that audits are costly to taxpayers. One reason to comply with the law is to not attract attention and reduce the likelihood of audits. When this motive for compliance is eliminated, the taxpayer may decide to pursue tax evasion more rather than less aggressively. Of course, in this case the probability of detection increases as well, and the net effect on compliance is unclear.

There is at least a possibility that a very high probability of audit (such as for large corporations that are almost continuously audited) can backfire when audits are themselves costly. According to Frey (1997), another way that auditing could backfire is by changing the motivation of taxpayers from intrinsic ("it's my duty to pay taxes") to extrinsic ("I pay because otherwise I'll get punished").

Fifth, Andreoni (1992) suggested that tax evasion may be pursued by taxpayers lacking easy access to credit. To the extent that this motive is important, an increased enforcement could potentially eliminate the role of the IRS as the lender of last resort and therefore reduce welfare.

It is sometimes suggested that tax considerations drive a lot of financial innovations. This is the sixth reason why tax avoidance may have some positive spillovers. While most of the financial products developed for avoidance purposes are likely not useful otherwise, there is a possibility that some of them turn out to have independent value but would not be invented otherwise.

Seventh, real-world tax systems are unlikely to be ideal. Addressing inefficiency of the tax system requires politically costly tax reform, and tax avoidance—letting well enough alone—may be a simple and practical way of addressing shortcomings of an inefficient tax structure. For example, suppose that, as much of the optimal taxation literature suggests, capital incomes should not be taxed, or should only be taxed lightly. In that case, the best policy response would be cutting tax rates imposed on capital income. If it is not politically feasible to pursue such policies explicitly, a similar outcome can be accomplished by reducing enforcement or increasing avoidance opportunities in this area. This is not how policy ought to be made, because a roundabout way of exempting capital income from taxation must be more costly than the explicit approach, but it may be better than preserving distortions present in the existing tax structure.

This is likely not an exhaustive list of potential positive side-effects of tax evasion and avoidance. These potential advantages do not provide automatic justifications for accepting non-compliance, but their existence suggests that understanding the side-effects of tax avoidance is relevant, and that benign neglect of certain types of tax avoidance can be a policy tool.

Some examples

Earned Income Tax Credit (EITC)

Of the slightly more than one million individual income tax returns audited by the IRS in 2004, almost 500,000 were for EITC recipients, resulting in an examination rate exceeding 4%, compared to 0.77% for all individual income tax returns (IRS 2005). EITC audits resulted in additional revenue of approximately $1.1 billion dollars, or about 18% of total discovered underpayments on the individual income tax returns. While examination of the return of an EITC claimant is likely to be much less costly than that of a high- income taxpayer,[15] the point remains that the IRS devotes very significant resources to enforcement related to this program. The question is whether this is a cost-effective use of these marginal enforcement dollar.

Efficiency in collecting revenue (or declining refunds) is clearly not the correct measure of enforcement impact, because it does not account for the deterrence effect. Still, on efficiency grounds the mere fact that substantial enforcement dollars are spent on the low-income population is puzzling. One of the original objectives of the Earned Income Tax Credit was to offset Social Security taxes. The credit grew over the years. With a phase-in rate of 40% for families with two children, for many its value now exceeds Social Security taxes. The fact remains that a large tax is paid on one side, and a large refund is received on the other. The world would have been simpler without low income taxpayers paying FICA taxes dur-

ing the year and receiving large refunds next April, with the associated enforcement problems on both sides.

Complexity is an important feature of the EITC. Taxpayers may
and do deal with complexity by hiring professional tax preparers. The
reliance on paid tax preparers grew in the 1990s. Most of the growth is
due to EITC filers increasing their reliance on professionals (Kopczuk
and Pop-Eleches 2005). This is one area where tax evasion attracted a
lot of attention because it indeed appears widespread, but this is also a
place where confusion caused by complexity is particularly visible.

As Holtzblatt and McCubbin (2004) discuss in detail, determining
eligibility for the EITC is not easy for a large number of low-income individuals. While things are relatively straightforward for a
two-parent family living with their children, for single, divorced,
separated parents or extended families, defining what a household
is, establishing whether a child is eligible for EITC purposes, and
determining who should claim the credit is far from trivial. The
compliance problem is further complicated due to inconsistency
between the EITC definition of the "qualifying child" and the eligibility rules for the dependent exemption and Child Tax Credit. Many
EITC claimants will be eligible for all three benefits.

Streamlining the definitions of a qualifying child used in the tax
code would be another natural area of improvement. There seems to be
no justification for having a child eligible for the purpose of claiming an
exemption but not for the EITC. The resulting reduction in taxpayers'
confusion would make it easier to assume that mistakes are in fact intentional and would therefore allow for more aggressive penalties, likely
resulting in higher compliance.

McCubbin (2000) cites evidence suggesting that examiners believed
that as much as 50% of EITC-related mistakes were unintentional.
Simultaneously, estimates of participation in the Earned Income Tax
Credit (e.g., Scholz 1994 IRS 2002; see also Holtzblatt and McCubbin
2004 for a concise summary of issues and findings) imply that about
20% of eligible individuals do not claim benefits, with higher estimates for subgroups such as new entrants to the labor market (Hill
et al. 1999). On the other hand, Kopczuk and Pop-Eleches (2005)
show that the EITC take-up increased as a result of an expansion of
the tax preparation industry (stimulated by higher profit opportunities due to electronic filing), and they discount the possibility that

the response is just due to increased cheating. They suggest that low-income taxpayers may have obtained access to a complexity-reducing technology—tax preparers—and responded by increasing participation. Alternatively, there could have been an increase in the visibility of the program driven by marketing efforts of the tax preparation industry. The latter could also be thought of as a special case of a reduction in complexity (from "I have no clue how the system works, and I didn't even know that the program existed" to some awareness of it).

The EITC is an example of a situation where mistakes and non-compliance problems run in both directions. Simultaneously there is cheating, honest confusion, and non-participation by eligible taxpayers. All of these problems owe something to the complexity of the tax code. Once complexity is reduced, pursuing fraud in the system would be much easier, while the objectives of the programs would be better served.

Deductions

Itemization creates a lot of tax avoidance opportunities by reducing the after-tax price of deductible activities. As such, it is likely to result in a higher elasticity of response to tax rates and therefore higher excess burden. This is mitigated by the fact that some deductible activities may indeed warrant lower tax rates, although an argument of this kind has to be made on a case-by-case basis. A number of deductions (for medical expenses, theft, and casualty losses) presumably adjust for a lower ability to pay. The basic optimal tax argument (Atkinson and Stiglitz 1976) would suggest that one needs to concentrate on the redistributive impact of such deductions *conditional* on the level of income: for example, given their level of income, are people who have high mortgage deductions or charitable contributions better or worse off? It is likely that this argument would go against subsidizing these activities. Furthermore, it is not at all clear why the preference for some of these activities should apply only at higher levels of income. Yet, this is precisely what happens, due to the allowance of a standard deduction.

From the complexity point of view, itemized deductions add a multitude of tax avoidance and evasion opportunities. They stimulate evasion by introducing into the tax code variables that are hard to monitor. They stimulate avoidance by introducing extra margins with differential tax treatment. The standard deduction in this context is a welcome means for reducing the complexity.

The Alternative Minimum Tax (AMT) plays a similar role by limiting deduction opportunities for people with higher income levels, including itemizable deductions. Three features of the AMT make it less effective though. First, from the taxpayer's point of view, the AMT calculation is implemented as a supplement to the individual income tax return. One has to explicitly figure out the difference between the regular income tax base and the alternative tax base. Computing taxable income directly, starting from the sources of income and allowable deductions, would be simpler from the taxpayer's point of view. Streamlining the computation would reduce the direct compliance cost, but it is unlikely to have much of an effect on the extent of avoidance and evasion other than, perhaps, reducing the likelihood of mistakes.

Second, while the AMT makes most of the deductions inframarginal[16] (good from the complexity point of view), it does so only *ex post*. At the beginning of the tax year, a taxpayer does not necessarily know whether she is going to be subject to the AMT because both future income and future deductions are uncertain. As a result, even if the AMT ends up applying *ex post*, *ex ante* one may be induced to engage in avoidance/evasion behavior. To some extent, this argument also applies to the standard deduction, but because a broader set of factors affect whether the AMT applies to an individual, predicting one's status is more of an issue in the AMT case.

Third, some deductions that are disallowed by the AMT have not much to do with tax sheltering. Examples are a deduction for state and local taxes and personal exemptions.

An effect similar to that of the AMT could be accomplished by simply capping the itemized deductions (or a subset of itemized deductions) using an appropriate threshold. It could be absolute in dollar terms, or it could mimic the current system more closely and avoid the danger of erosion by inflation by being set proportional to taxpayers' adjusted gross income. With a little bit of effort, one could also envision a similar change for the disallowed income preference items. This would make the whole calculation more transparent, would therefore reduce the *ex ante* uncertainty in tax planning, and likely reduce the direct compliance cost.

Tax preparers and software

More than 60% of personal income tax returns in the United States are prepared by paid tax preparers. Most of the remaining ones, while prepared by taxpayers themselves, rely on tax software. This pattern suggests that certain aspects of filing that are commonly considered to add complexity are less relevant in practice. This applies in particular to computing one's tax liability. When a tax preparer or software does this computation for the taxpayer, progressivity of the tax code—the use of multiple tax brackets and rates—no longer imposes any extra burden on the taxpayer. Neither do other features of the tax code, such as separate computations of taxes on dividends or capital gains or the phase-outs of various benefits.

The role of tax preparers is less clear. A large number of options available to taxpayers makes it worthwhile to hire a professional who can help in identifying the most promising course of action. However, it is unlikely that outright tax evasion is facilitated by tax preparers. This is because the financial reward from cheating on the tax return accrues mostly to the taxpayer, but penalties are much harsher on tax preparers; in particular, criminal prosecution is more common. A tax preparer may have a better understanding of how the IRS operates, and therefore be more realistic about the risks involved. As a result, tax preparers might choose to pursue different avoidance and evasion strategies than taxpayers would pick themselves.

Blumenthal and Christian (2004) provide a short survey of the literature of the impact of tax preparers on compliance. Identifying the effect is difficult because the decision to hire a tax preparer is endogenous, and furthermore the choice of a particular type of tax preparer is endogenous (Erard 1993). Evidence on this topic is scarce, but does not point to tax preparers systematically increasing non-compliance.

From the point of view of the IRS, reliance on tax preparers should be welcome. As mentioned before, one way of increasing enforcement—penalties—is threatened by the importance of unintentional mistakes that taxpayers make. The likelihood of such mistakes falls when a tax professional is involved, thus reducing the likelihood that penalties will be imposed on otherwise honest taxpayers. This makes it possible to increase penalties. Harsh penalties can be (and are) imposed on tax preparers, thereby increasing the likelihood that they do not, in fact, facilitate tax evasion. Because a tax preparer deals with many customers, the IRS can more easily identify clusters of cheating by identifying preparers who systematically file fraudulent returns.

This is not to say that devoting attention to preparers solves the compliance problem. As argued above, tax preparers may facilitate tax avoidance, and not much can be done when the promoted strategy is legal. Tax preparers also have to rely on information provided to them by taxpayers, and there is little that can be done if a taxpayer chooses to withhold it. A tax preparer cannot, of course, play the role of an auditor without facing a risk of losing business. The IRS could remedy this by mandating all tax preparers to behave in the same way. For example, the IRS could impose requirements on tax preparers (and penalties in case of discrepancies) to verify information that currently need not be reported to the IRS (such as the purchase price of an asset) or that is currently not verified by the IRS. On top of the direct effect, strategies of this kind would make it harder to rely on a paid professional and still cheat. As a result, taxpayers who do cheat would be more likely to file on their own, making self-filers a natural target for audits.

Phase-ins and phase-outs
Recent tax reforms included a multitude of phase-ins and phase-outs of various tax provisions. This is a natural example of the kind of undesirable complexity stressed here. By legislating predictably different tax treatments of the same activity in subsequent years, it creates an opportunity for successful tax planning by, for example, retiming realization of income or shifting deductions to years when their tax treatment is more beneficial. While much planning of that kind is not illegal, it does amount to an extra loss of revenue beyond legislation's intended effects. This loss is costly because it requires either keeping other tax rates higher or running debt (and increasing future taxes).

From the point of view of individual taxpayers, there are a few additional costs. First, there is a cost of implementing a particular method of shifting income across years with different tax treatment. Second, there is an extra risk because future policies are uncertain; for example, many of the 2001 Bush tax cuts were accelerated in 2003.[17] Third, this kind of tax policy has made the tax system much less transparent. Taxpayers cannot rely on their experience because the law does in fact change from one year to the next. They may also assume that tax provisions that they took advantage of last year apply this year as well, when in reality they do not. The resulting confusion increases the likelihood of mistakes and therefore, as previously argued, makes standard enforcement much harder.

Conclusions

This chapter has presented an overview of policy implications of tax complexity from an economic perspective. It suggested that tax evasion and tax avoidance are similarly costly from the social point of view, despite differences in their legal status. A comprehensive compliance policy should target both. While penalties and increased probability of detection are the main tools of targeting tax evasion, a reduction in complexity of the tax code would reduce opportunities for both tax evasion and tax avoidance, and it would additionally make penalties a more viable policy choice.

Complexity in the tax code should be thought of as the extent of variation in possible tax treatments of economically related activities. This kind of complexity naturally creates opportunities for tax avoidance, and it also causes difficulties for otherwise honest taxpayers. As a result, it leads to confusion and mistakes that are often hard to distinguish from dishonesty. Consequently, penalties become a less appealing approach to enforcement while, simultaneously, detection becomes more costly. From this perspective, efforts of the IRS to educate taxpayers and provide better customer service are a reasonable compliance approach, because they increase the effectiveness of the standard enforcement tools of penalties and audits.

Several methods of reducing complexity have been briefly discussed. Reliance on the standard deduction and capping deductions or preferences is one approach to making the tax code simpler for many taxpayers. An increased reliance on commercial tax preparers allows for a reduced likelihood of unintentional mistakes and, while it does not eliminate the complexity of the tax code, it reduces confusion and makes standard enforcement more effective. It also allows for shifting some of the enforcement focus to the tax preparation sector, which is arguably easier to target than individual taxpayers. Two examples of questionable complexity that were highlighted were the eligibility criteria in the EITC and the use of phase-in and phase-out provisions.

Policy makers are unlikely to stop experimenting with the tax code. Some aspects of special tax provisions are fairly well understood: there is a direct revenue cost as well as the potential response of the affected and related activities. What is not sufficiently appreciated is that any provision of this kind adds to complexity in the tax code. This effect is hard to quantify, but its implications are real. New and innovative avoidance strategies are hard to predict. The increased cost of enforcement is also difficult to quantify. We also have no direct way of measuring the effect on unintentional mistakes. Slemrod and Kopczuk (2002) suggest that the first of these effects will show up as an increased elasticity of response to taxation and therefore higher marginal excess burden. There is no progress so far on the other two. Building an economic framework that allows for measuring the costs due to a marginal increase in complexity is a necessary input for understanding the full impact of specialized tax provisions.

The main point is that the costs of complexity go far beyond the direct compliance costs in the form of time or money that are imposed on taxpayers struggling to understand and comply with the tax law. While such direct costs are undoubtedly important, in practice, complexity also breeds opportunities for successful tax planning. Hence, complexity generates distortions; it makes the effective tax treatment of related activities different. Complexity also results in inequities because otherwise similar taxpayers end up with different tax burdens, simply because their willingness to exploit the law varies, or opportunities to do so vary. Moreover, complexity creates confusion and in the presence of confused taxpayers, enforcement is more difficult and less effective. Tax collectors have to sort through more non-compliance cases and, unless one is willing to punish honest taxpayers, they also have to spend resources on distinguishing between mischief and error.

The preferred way of dealing with compliance problems is fixing the tax code. When taxpayers can no longer easily claim confusion, what is left on the table will be noncompliance by cheaters, thereby allowing the IRS to enforce free of distraction.

Endnotes

1.   A loss of welfare occurs if there is a way to allocate the same resources in a way that makes a taxpayer better off. For example, in the context of tax evasion, a taxpayer would be made better off by receiving the expected gain from tax evasion directly rather taking a risk.

2.   A tax distortion is a provision of the tax code that can influence a taxpayer's behavior, over and above the fact of taxation itself. Insofar as a tax alters the taxpayer's behavior, his new circumstances are less advantageous than previously, and the extent of this disadvantage is known as the deadweight loss from taxation. For instance, if a cigarette tax causes one to smoke less, the difference in the individual's well-being implied by the switch is an economic cost, apart from the tax he actually pays. The tax paid is not a loss to society, since it is merely transferred from taxpayer to government. The deadweight loss is an economic cost to society. At the same time, the public services financed by the tax could provide benefits that exceed those of whatever the tax money would have been used to purchase by the taxpayer.

3.   By referring to efficiency I have in mind how resources are allocated to various productive uses. This is conceptually separate than a concern about equity or fairness. By referring to efficiency I also place no independent value on taxpayers being honest (although, to the extent that increased honesty has an effect on behavior of other taxpayers, it could indirectly affect how efficiently resources are allocated).

4.   The excess burden of taxation is the extra welfare loss over the revenue collected by the government. The marginal excess burden refers to the incremental change in the excess burden due to a small change in tax rates. The marginal excess burden (or, more precisely, the marginal cost of funds discussed later in the chapter) is both the measure of the cost of increasing the reliance on a particular type of taxation and the measure of the cost of collecting more revenue.

5.   No such instruments should have an effect on a rational taxpayer, but a growing literature on behavioral economics argues that deviation from economic rationality may be important.

6.   There is some ambiguity in this definition. The actual amount of tax savings may be risky under tax avoidance if the underlying activity is risky. For example, a taxpayer who chooses to realize capital gains does not know the exact magnitude of tax savings because they depend on future appreciation. Tax avoidance by deferring taxes involves uncertainty about future taxes, but the risk is not under control of the tax collection agency.

7.   Note that tax deferral also falls here. For example, realization-based taxes treat investment strategies with different frequency of trading differentially.

8.   The tax gap was estimated to decline a little bit more (0.2-0.3%) by 1992, however these estimates were projections based on the same data source (1988 TCMP) and therefore do not provide new information about the actual change in compliance but only about the composition of tax base (which may itself be affected by compliance).

9.   This is not to say that vertical inequity due to tax avoidance is not important. My view is, however, that redistributional implications of tax avoidance should be analyzed jointly with other policy instruments and such a discussion is, for the most part, beyond

the scope of this chapter. For an example of such a discussion, see Kesselman (1997). I also do not tackle the issue of incidence of evasion and avoidance (see, for example, Kesselman 1989).

10. More precisely, the value of government's dollar (ignoring distributional concerns) is given by the marginal cost of funds (MFC) and is defined as the ratio of the effect of change in the tax rate on the revenue absent behavioral response over the revenue effect accounting for behavioral responses (see, for example, Slemrod and Yitzhaki 2002). A government's dollar is more costly than a private one (even if the MCF is less than one) as long as substitution effects due to increased taxes act to reduce revenue. This is because the social value of a private dollar is equal to the value of a lump-sum transfer and therefore it is affected by income effects on the revenue, but not by substitution effects.

11. The elasticity of income refers to the effect of a 1% change in the tax price (one minus the marginal tax rate) on the level of income, expressed in percentage terms. Reported income refers to the total income reported on the tax return while taxable income refers to the actual income subject to taxation (after suitable deductions and exemptions have been subtracted). The elasticity of taxable income is the key parameter underlying the calculation of the cost of the income tax (Feldstein 1995, 1999).

12. Elasticity is formally defined as the percent change in one variable, given a 1% change in a related variable. It's a way to measure the response of something to a given change in something else. For instance, if a 1% increase in an hourly wage causes the worker to work half a percent more hours, the elasticity of hours worked with respect to the wage is one-half.

In this context, the elasticity of taxable income with respect to the tax base is the percentage change in taxable income, given a 1% change in the size of the tax base. The broadness of the tax system was measured as a fraction of income reported on the tax return that was ultimately subject to taxation, with itemized deductions, exclusions, and adjustments making up the difference.

13. Preliminary estimates based on the 2001 National Research Program are available at the IRS Web site as "Tax Gap Facts and Figures," accessed on October 3rd at http://www.irs.gov/pub/irs-utl/tax_gap_facts-figures.pdf. Estimates for 1985, 1988, and 1992 (based on 1988 TCMP and earlier ones) are in IRS (1996). The overall patterns are quite similar.

14. The non-compliance rate was defined as the gross tax gap divided by sum of the gross tax gap and "voluntarily and timely paid" taxes. An alternative definition would replace the numerator by the (necessarily smaller) net tax gap that further accounts for enforcement revenue. Using this definition and the data from sources cited in the text, the non-compliance rate was 15.3-15.6% in 1985, 13.6-13.8% in 1988, 14.2-14.6% in 1992, and 12.4-14.1% in 2001.

15. In fact, almost 95% of below-$25,000 tax filers were examined by compliance centers without a need to send an agent, while the corresponding number for all income tax returns is just 80%. It also seems safe to assume that the qualifications of an examiner inspecting EITC cases may be much lower than average. The costs associated with the Earned Income Tax Credit in 2004 were on the order of $200 million, relative to an almost $4 billion enforcement budget (IRS 2005, table 30).

16.   Inframarginal in general means below the surface, or short of some kind of boundary.   In economic terms, a change "on the margin" means an incremental change in one factor, such as the tax rate, and some possible resulting change in whatever is subject to tax.   An inframarginal change in taxes is one that is not affected by taxpayer response.   If for instance a taxpayer is in the 15% bracket, a change in the 10% bracket that altered his tax liability would not be affected by his response.   In the context of the AMT, by eliminating some deductions, changes in behavior related to those deductions are no longer influenced by the income tax.

17.   This is a cost imposed even on those who do not wish to engage in tax avoidance because it amounts to uncertainty about disposable income.

References

Akerlof, George A. 1978. The economics of 'tagging' as applied to optimal income tax, welfare programs, and manpower planning. *American Economic Review.* Vol. 68, No. 1, pp.8-19. March.

Allingham, Michael G. and Agnar Sandmo. 1972. Income tax evasion: A theoretical analysis. *Journal of Public Economics.* Vol. 1, No. 3-4, pp. 323-38. November.

Andreoni, James. 1992. IRS as loan-shark: Tax compliance with borrowing constraints. *Journal of Public Economics.* Vol. 49, No. 1, pp. 35-46. October.

Atkinson, Anthony B. and Joseph E. Stiglitz. 1976. The design of tax structure: Direct versus indirect taxation. *Journal of Public Economics.* Vol. 6, No. 1-2, pp. 55-75. July-August.

Auerbach, Alan J. and Kevin A. Hassett. 2002. A new measure of horizontal equity. *American Economic Review.* Vol. 92, No. 2, pp. 1116-25. September.

Baldry, Jonathan C. 1984. The enforcement of income tax laws: Efficiency implications. *Economic Record.* Vol. 60, pp. 156-59. June.

Becker, Gary S. 1968. Crime and punishment: An economic approach. *Journal of Political Economy.* Vol. 76, No. 2, pp. 169-217. January/ February.

Becker, Gary S. and Casey B. Mulligan. 2003. Deadweight costs and the size of government. *Journal of Law and Economics.* Vol. 46, No. 2, pp. 293-340. October.

Blumenthal, Marsha and Charles Christian. 2004. "Tax Preparers." In Henry J. Aaron and Joel Slemrod, eds., *The Crisis in Tax Administration.* Washington, D.C.: Brookings Institution Press.

Erard, Brian. 1993. Taxation with representation: An analysis of the role of tax practitioners in tax compliance. *Journal of Public Economics.* Vol. 52. No. 2, pp. 163-97. September.

Erard, Brian and Chih-Chin Ho. 2001. Searching for ghosts: Who are nonfilers and how much tax do they owe? *Journal of Public Economics.* Vol. 81, No. 1, pp. 25-50. July.

Feldstein, Martin S. 1995. The effect of marginal tax rates on taxable income: A panel study of the 1986 Tax Reform Act. *Journal of Political Economy.* Vol. 103, No. 3, pp. 551-72. June.

Feldstein, Martin S. 1999. Tax avoidance and the deadweight loss of the income tax. *Review of Economics and Statistics.* Vol. 81, No. 4, pp. 674-80. November.

Frey, Bruno. 1997. Constitution for knaves crowds out civic virtues. *Economic Journal.* Vol. 107, pp. 1043-53.

Gordon, Roger, Laura Kalambokidis, and Joel Slemrod. 2004. Do we now collect any revenue from taxing capital income? *Journal of Public Economics.* Vol. 88, No. 5, pp. 981-1009. April.

Gordon, Roger and Joel Slemrod. 1988. "Do We Collect Any Revenue from Taxing Capital Income?" In Lawrence Summers, ed, *Tax Policy and the Economy.* Cambridge, Mass.: MIT Press and National Bureau of Economic Research. pp. 89-130.

Gruber, Jonathan and Emmanuel Saez. 2002. The elasticity of taxable income: evidence and implications. *Journal of Public Economics.* Vol. 84, No. 1, pp. 1-32. April.

Hill, Carolyn J., V. Joseph Hotz, Charles H. Mullin, and John Karl Scholz. 1999. EITC eligibility, participation and compliance rates for AFDC households: Evidence from the California caseload. Mimeo. April.

Holtzblatt, Janet and Janet McCubbin. 2004. "Issues Affecting Low-Income Filers." In Henry J. Aaron and Joel Slemrod, eds., *The Crisis in Tax Administration.* Washington, D.C.: Brookings Institution Press.

Internal Revenue Service. 1996. Federal tax compliance research. *Individual Income Tax Gap Estimates for 1985, 1988 and 2002.* Publication 1415 (Rev 4-96).

Internal Revenue Service. 2002. Participation in the Earned Income Tax Credit Program for tax year 1996. Research Project 12.26. U.S. Department of Treasury. January 31.

Internal Revenue Service. 2005a. *Internal Revenue Service Data Book 2004.* Publication 55B. Washington, D.C. March.

Internal Revenue Service. 2005b. Understanding the tax gap. IRS Fact Sheet, #FS-2005-14. March. Accessed online on October 25, 2005 at http://www.irs.gov/newsroom/article/0,,id=137246,00.html.

Kesselman, Jonathan R. 1989. Income tax evasion: Intersectoral analysis. *Journal of Public Economics.* Vol. 38, No. 2, pp. 137-82. March.

Kesselman, Jonathan R. 1997. "Policy Implications of Tax Evasion and the Underground Economy." In Owen Lippert and Michael Walker eds., *The Underground Economy: Global Evidence of Its Size and Impact,* Vancouver, BC, Canada: The Fraser Institute.

Kopczuk, Wojciech. 2001. Redistribution when avoidance behavior is heterogeneous. *Journal of Public Economics.* July. Vol. 81, No, 1, pp. 51-71.

Kopczuk, Wojciech. 2005. Tax bases, tax rates and the elasticity of reported income. *Journal of Public Economics.* Vol. 89, No. 11-12, pp. 2093-2119. December.

Kopczuk, Wojciech and Cristian Pop-Eleches. 2005. "Electronic filing, tax preparers and participation in the Earned Income Tax Credit." Working Paper 11768. National Bureau of Economic Research. November.

Liebman, Jeffrey B. and Richard Zeckhauser. 2005. "Schmeduling." Harvard University. Mimeo.

Mayshar, Joram. 1991. Taxation with costly administration. *Scandinavian Journal of Economics.* Vol. 93, No. 1, pp. 75-88.

McCubbin, Janet. 2000. EITC noncompliance: The determinants of misreporting of children. *National Tax Journal.* Vol. 53, No. 4, Part 2, pp. 135-1164. December.

Saez, Emmanuel. 2004. "Reported Incomes and Marginal Tax Rates, 1960-2000: Evidence and Policy Implications." In James Poterba, ed., *Tax Policy and Economy*. Vol. 18.

Schmalbeck, Richard. 2001. "Avoiding Federal Wealth Transfer Taxes." In William G. Gale, James R. Hines Jr., and Joel Slemrod, eds., *Rethinking Estate and Gift Taxation.* Washington, D.C.: Brookings Institution Press.

Scholz, John Karl. 1994. The Earned Income Tax Credit: participation, compliance and anit-roverty effectiveness. *National Tax Journal.* Vol. 48, No. 1, pp. 59-81. March.

Scotchmer Suzanne and Joel Slemrod. 1989. Randomness in tax enforcement. *Journal of Public Economics.* Vol. 38, No. 1, pp. 17-32. February.

Sillamaa, Mary Anne and Michael R. Veall. 2001. The effect of marginal tax rates on taxable income: A panel study of the 1988 tax flattening in Canada. *Journal of Public Economics.* Vol. 80, No. 3, pp. 341-56. June.

Slemrod, Joel. 1994. Fixing the leak in the Okun's bucket: Optimal progressivity when avoidance can be controlled. *Journal of Public Economics.* Vol. 55, No. 1, pp. 41-51. September.

Slemrod, Joel, Marsha Blumenthal, and Charles Christian. 2001. Taxpayer response to an increased probability of audit: Evidence from a controlled experiment in Minnesota. *Journal of Public Economics.* Vol. 79, No. 3, pp. 455-83. March.

Slemrod, Joel and Wojciech Kopczuk. 2002. The optimal elasticity of taxable income. *Journal of Public Economics.* Vol. 84, No. 1, pp. 91-112. April.

Slemrod, Joel and Shlomo Yitzhaki. 2002. "Tax Avoidance, Evasion and Administration." In Alan J. Auerbach and Martin S. Feldstein, eds., *Handbook of Public Economics (Vol. 3).* Holland: Elsevier.

Steuerle, Eugene. 2005a. Improved information reporting for capital gains. *Tax Notes.* pp. 697-98. August 8.

Steuerle, Eugene. 2005b. Expanded information reporting for charitable contributions. *Tax Notes.* pp. 813-14. August 15.

Stiglitz, Joseph. 1985. The general theory of tax avoidance. *National Tax Journal.* September. Vol. 38, No. 3, pp. 325-37.

Triest, Robert. 1992. The effect of income taxation on labor supply when deductions are endogenous. *Review of Economics and Statistics.* Vol. 74, No. 1, pp. 91-99. February.

Yitzhaki, Shlomo. 1974. A note on income tax evasion: A theoretical analysis. *Journal of Public Economics.* Vol. 69, No. 2, pp. 201-02. May.

About EPI

The Economic Policy Institute was founded in 1986 to widen the debate about policies to achieve healthy economic growth, prosperity, and opportunity.

In the United States today, inequality in wealth, wages, and income remains historically high. Expanding global competition, changes in the nature of work, and rapid technological advances are altering economic reality. Yet many of our policies, attitudes, and institutions are based on assumptions that no longer reflect real world conditions.

With the support of leaders from labor, business, and the foundation world, the Institute has sponsored research and public discussion of a wide variety of topics: trade and fiscal policies; trends in wages, incomes, and prices; education; the causes of the productivity slowdown; labor market problems; rural and urban policies; inflation; state-level economic development strategies; comparative international economic performance; and studies of the overall health of the U.S. manufacturing sector and of specific key industries.

The Institute works with a growing network of innovative economists and other social science researchers in universities and research centers in the U.S. and abroad who are willing to go beyond the conventional wisdom in considering strategies for public policy.

Founding scholars of the Institute include Jeff Faux, distinguished fellow and former president of EPI; Lester Thurow, Sloan School of Management, MIT; Ray Marshall, former U.S. secretary of labor, professor at the LBJ School of Public Affairs, University of Texas; Barry Bluestone, Northeastern University; Robert Reich, former U.S. secretary of labor; and Robert Kuttner, author, editor of *The American Prospect,* and columnist for *Business Week* and the Washington Post Writers Group.

For additional information about the Institute, contact EPI at 1333 H Street NW, Suite 300, East Tower, Washington, DC 20005, (202) 775-8810, or visit www.epi.org.